THE REFLECTIVE LEARNER
Seeing 'Missed Takes' in Mistakes

Compiled & Edited by Neeraja Raghavan
Foreword Kamala V Mukunda

A THINKING TEACHER
Publication

Thinking Teacher

notionpress
.com

INDIA · SINGAPORE · MALAYSIA

Notion Press

Old No. 38, New No. 6
McNichols Road, Chetpet
Chennai - 600 031

First Published by Notion Press 2019
ⓒ Neeraja Raghavan 2019

ISBN 978-1-64678-801-9

Cover Photograph: K Natarajan, Rishi Valley School
Cover Design: GVR Rajeshwar, Rishi Valley School

CONTENTS

ACKNOWLEDGEMENTS

I owe several people a debt of gratitude for the work that has been compiled in this book.

Kamala Mukunda responded with swift alacrity to my tentative request to write the Foreword. Her enthusiastic response and warm encouragement mean a lot to me.

To the School Heads of Poorna Learning Centre, Taktse International School and The Peepal Grove School, I owe gratitude for allowing me to engage with their teachers and intrude into their school spaces whenever needed. Had it not been for their openness and confidence in the Reflective Learner Programme, this book would not have been possible.

The four teachers who conducted this research were as meticulous as they were patient: for their work has been put together long after they completed it. I owe them thanks – both for giving me the privilege of facilitating their work, as well as never once asking me when their papers would see the light of day! I can only hope that the final production in this form makes up somewhat for keeping them waiting!

Natarajan was generous with his superb photographs which are always very difficult to select from: each one is such a masterpiece! He worked patiently with the Cover Designer, Rajeshwar, to produce the cover and never once complained about my numerous suggestions to tweak it here, or change it there. Rajeshwar submitted design after design without a murmur: to both these gentlemen, I owe warm thanks.

Sita Natarajan read through the raw manuscript and spotted many edits which slipped my eye. I thank her for taking the time to do this.

Nidhi Pant was as skilful as always: her copy-editing is about the best that I have experienced! Thank you, Nidhi, for always being ready to rally around!

Ramakumar and Vidhya Nagaraj responded with readiness and generosity to my request for evidence that students can reflect. I thank them both for sharing the excerpts that they did.

The students who participated in this research are the most important people to thank: for without them, none of this work could have been carried out. I owe them my deep gratitude. But for the solid support extended to me by Ludy and Narayan, this book would not have come out. Thank you, Ludy and Narayan!

And finally, I thank you, dear reader, for imposing your faith in this work by taking the time to read it. I look forward to your valuable feedback.

FOREWORD

You are holding in your hands an unusual gem of a book.

As you read, you will meet and get to know four enthusiastic teachers, and discover what makes them tick at work. Their interest in how children learn is revealed in the way they explore their students' *mistakes.* Instead of flagging these mistakes with red crosses and then just forgetting all about them, these four teachers begin a new journey of learning sparked off by the different kinds of errors that students tend to make in their English and mathematics classes. The book details their explorations into learning, and has all the strengths of the case study method, with its meticulous attention to the micro-steps along the way. The writing is very tight and concise, mercifully free of hand-waving and glib prescriptions. Its twin goals – of opening our eyes to the pedagogical value of mistakes, and of showcasing the exciting potential of action research by teachers – are admirably met.

The idea that mistakes can and should provide insights that feed back into our teaching is, at one level, so obviously true. However, it is not at all a prevalent practice. Mistakes usually only contribute to the overall score on an assignment or a test, and therefore only serve to place students on a continuum of performance. Teaching goes on, oblivious of the mistaken thought processes going on in the child's mind, even though these thoughts are bound to form the basis for further learning. In the next round of testing and scoring, the student once again makes mistakes and is evaluated in a repeating cycle of misunderstandings. Here in this book, Prerna, Gopi, Michael and

Kanchana simply and without fuss demonstrate all that is possible when a teacher adopts a radically different approach towards mistakes.

As a teacher of more than 25 years myself, I know that it is immensely rewarding to share one's teaching ideas with others. It extends the scope of our work, to know that others can use our ideas and benefit from our hard work. It is a gift to both the teachers and their readers that Neeraja has nurtured this book into being, richly peppered with usable rubrics, worksheets and activities. Behind the good ideas written about here, you can sense the almost invisible hand of the mentor. One wishes as one reads that every teacher had a mentor like this in their pocket – someone to bounce ideas off, to share success stories with, and occasionally, on whose shoulder to cry!

The four teachers' enthusiasm is palpable and infectious, but more important than enthusiasm are certain key qualities that they have in common. I explain below the three most important qualities according to me. It is easy to miss these, or take them for granted because they have not been pointed out explicitly, and I feel it would be a pity not to acknowledge them.

- ✦ They have all created non-threatening environments for their students. This is no minor achievement. There are indications throughout the book of how much effort is put into reassuring children and giving them the confidence to acknowledge mistakes to both teacher and peers, learning together from them.
- ✦ They are fascinated by the learning mind. I found it striking that the word psychology is everywhere present in the book, but never mentioned (except as part of a referenced title!). The whole endeavour of exploring students' errors is deeply psychological: 'entering students' minds', as one of the teachers puts it. The book is in some ways the best endorsement for the methods and subject of psychology that one can ask for.
- ✦ They willingly put in 'extra' hours to get all their students to make their work excellent. Yet, chock-full of ideas as the book is, it also respects your time as a teacher. There is the clear

acknowledgement that a teacher's time is precious, even as it is acknowledged that teaching is not a 9-5 job.

Two things are sure to happen as you read this book (both happened to me).

First, you will itch to try something or the other out in your own class. I am planning to try Gopi's 'next step' worksheet in a maths class, and Michael's 'find this error' correction method for my senior students' psychology essays, among other ideas. Second, you will itch to share something from here with a fellow-teacher – I want to tell my colleagues about Kanchana's error classification scheme, and Prerna's discoveries about the benefits of simple one-on-one time with a struggling student. I must, however, wait patiently for the book to be published before I can do all this, but by the time you the reader are reading this sentence, I will have scratched both itches and had my way!

Kamala V. Mukunda
Bangalore, 2019

Whether you think you can or think you can't - you are right.

Popularly attributed to Henry Ford

PREFACE

This book contains narratives of a voluntary journey undertaken by four teachers in different schools located in the Indian states of Karnataka, Andhra Pradesh and Sikkim.

Each of these teachers had a desire to connect more deeply with their students, particularly those students who were seen to be 'struggling'. All four of them also felt the need to understand the rationale behind the mistakes made by these students. In their exploration, these teachers embarked on an initiative called the Reflective Learner Programme.

As the narratives contained in this book reveal, these initially 'struggling' students underwent remarkable transformation over the course of the programme: from disinterested and unmotivated learners, they transformed into enthusiastic and successful students – sometimes, within a few months. More significantly, as they began to examine the workings of their own minds, their repetitive erroneous habits and thinking patterns surfaced, which they were themselves able to see. Slowly, they began to address them – in the beginning,

From Minutes to Months

On an ordinary day, a seemingly innocuous document landed in my inbox. Sent by Kamala Anilkumar, a retired teacher in Mysore, it summarised one of the many Parent Teacher Meetings that Kamala had anchored during her more-than-two-decade stint at The School, KFI (Chennai). Titled 'Looking at Mistakes', it included some questions around the same theme that the parents and teachers had discussed (during this meeting):

✦ Why do children find it easier to admit to mistakes than adults?
✦ Why do children make fewer mistakes on the games field than in the classroom?
✦ Why do we often repeat the same mistakes?

In less than five minutes, I was struck by the enormous potential of such enquiry.

From a document that included 'mere' minutes of a meeting, it took a few months for Kamala, Vineeta Sood (contributing editor of *The Reflective Teacher*) and me to design the Reflective Learner Programme that is described in this book.

with the teacher's support, and then, on their own. This swiftly led to their breaking free of the shackles of limiting beliefs like 'I can never get it', and their enhanced levels of self-confidence were soon palpable.

While teachers began to reduce the one-on-one time that they had been spending with the students (to analyse their error patterns), students gradually began to carry out this exercise themselves. Students who could not figure out why something was 'wrong' now became the very ones who could identify – and even fix – their errors, *on their own*. Some of them articulated their enhanced levels of self-confidence ('I never knew that I was so creative!') and showed visible signs of enjoying the same subject that they had earlier been afraid of.

At the same time, teachers, too, began to look at mistakes in a more nuanced fashion: beyond just 'right' and 'wrong'. One teacher discovered that as students begin to write more complex sentences, the number of errors is bound to go up: and this indicates the greater self-confidence in the student *who is now willing to try writing complex sentences*. Another confessed that her own image of a student (as being indifferent) had been sensed by the student ('The child knew it') and thus, the student lived up to this image. No sooner did the teacher revisit her own assumption about this child, than *the child began to sense this, too* – and changed in a very short period of time to being far more motivated and showing visible interest in learning. In another instance, just by a teacher's positive re-enforcement, a notoriously slow child whose time management skills were abysmal changed in less than three months to one who managed his time very well.

Thus, using the oft-made errors of each student as the doorway to understanding the workings of that student's mind, these teachers slowly moved to a totally new vantage point from where they had started. They gradually began to look at the 'struggling' students with new respect, even as they began to reflect more deeply on their own beliefs, assumptions and pedagogical strategies.

Indeed, by the end of the programme, not just the students but teachers, too, became reflective learners.

Audience

This book is meant for a broad spectrum of readers.

Parents who wish to understand why their children sometimes struggle with the curriculum will find some insights herein. Teachers who are caught up in the day-to-day rush of 'covering the syllabus' – while they push aside that gnawing discontent – may well find ways to identify the cause of such discontent and then release themselves from it. Students who feel overwhelmed by the enormous content that they are expected to master – and are dissatisfied with their progress – can draw inspiration from some of the narratives in this book and move forward with greater motivation. Principals of schools and colleges can explore the possibility of introducing such a programme in their institutions, so as to resist the compulsion to adopt a 'one-size-fits-all' approach and, instead, examine ways and means of individualising learning.

Flow of the Book

Beginning with a broad introduction that sets this work against a backdrop of research in this domain, this book contains four chapters that describe the action research carried out by the respective teachers. One of the four teachers chose to write out her work like a formal research paper, while the other three chose a less formal route of sharing their notes with the facilitator – who later turned these into the narratives contained in this book. These narratives also include a brief profile of the teacher-researcher, as each chapter takes the reader through the journey of sensitising students (and getting sensitised, as a teacher) to the immense learning that lies behind each mistake.

Despite the apparent asymmetry in the layout of the four chapters, the different styles (three non-formal, one formal) have been deliberately retained, in order to showcase to readers different choices that are available for a teacher to document such work.

A concluding chapter summarises each teacher's efforts through a flow chart that depicts the route employed by each teacher-researcher, thus offering the reader a bird's eye view of the entire process. In addition, it highlights a couple of other possibilities for teachers and School Principals to draw out reflective learning from their students.

Above all, by the end of this book, it is hoped that every reader will appreciate – at least to some degree – the tremendous impact of an atmosphere that is free from judgement and shame in committing mistakes, the need to acknowledge and utilise the enormous learning opportunities that are embedded in each mistake and the incredible value in respecting and honouring the erring learner.

The greatest mistake you can make in life is to be continually fearing you will make a mistake.

Elbert Hubbard

INTRODUCTION

BRINGING MISTAKES INTO THE CURRICULUM

Traditionally, education (in Indian schools and colleges) aims to help the learner excel in the subjects taught: *by getting things right.* The commonest mindset is one which holds that erroneous understanding should be looked down upon, and the 'wrong answer' should be abhorred. Even where mistakes are not deemed shameful, they are frequently seen as avoidable, and worse, are sometimes left undisclosed. Even if one errs, one should, somehow, quickly correct the mistake and move on, as far as possible. Repeated occurrence of the same mistake – what we refer to as 'error patterns' – is condemned as being symptomatic of the learner 'not being up to the mark', or 'not showing an aptitude for the subject'. Acknowledging one's mistakes is therefore not easy – in such a climate that condemns the very making of one.

It was the experience of the teacher-researchers who undertook this research that mistakes open up a whole new world of metacognitive learning: a learner who is aware of his/her own erroneous understanding will be better equipped to address it, than one who pushes his/her mistakes under the rug. Such awareness cannot flower in an ambience that discourages the making of mistakes. In such a climate, all that can happen is a hesitant and diffident back-and-forth movement between understanding and confusion, as errors sprout in their minds and then retreat in diffidence again. In the worst case, the young learner withdraws from learning if errors consistently abound.

Philosophers such as John Dewey, Bertrand Russell, Karl Popper and John Stuart Mill have all pointed out that mistakes are often an inevitable aspect of human activity and inquiry (Swartz 1976). Popper (1962) wrote: 'We can learn from our mistakes', and, followed this up with the statement: 'All our knowledge grows only through the correcting of our mistakes.' A. F. Chalmers (1973) has qualified this by proposing that we learn effectively from our mistakes by being cautious. While it is widely accepted (in theory) that mistakes are doorways to more effective learning, there are hardly any recorded instances in India (Gangola et al. 2011 is one) of academicians actually bringing this practice into the curriculum.

Internationally, however, some headway has been made in this domain. Several educators have worked in the area of looking at mistakes across disciplines spanning literature, mathematics and social work. For instance, while teaching literature, B. S. Locklin (2013) discovered that just by looking at errors differently, a great deal of learning emerged for both the teacher as well as the learners. This held true, Locklin found, even if the error was merely one of simple miscomprehension – as 'a student's misreading can reveal something important about the text, allowing all of us to question assumptions'.

The power in examining a mistake is repeatedly stressed by researchers like J. Sconyers (1976) who exemplifies it in mathematics, by listing several important learnings that emerged purely by virtue of starting with a mistaken hypothesis in matrix algebra. The realisation of this mistake opened the door 'for healthy caution for conclusions reached inductively and hasty generalisations' and also enhanced 'respect for the power of deductive reasoning'. As Sconyers asserts: 'We learned that mistakes aren't necessarily "bad". In fact, in our case, without the original mistaken hypothesis we'd never have achieved anything!'

Social work researchers have been inducted into looking at the mistakes of others in order to learn from them, by examining the issue of scientific misconduct with a view to prevention (Gibelman and Gelman 2001) of unethical or illegal practices. Thus, there is a plethora of literature spanning inadvertent and comprehension errors; identifying illogical deductions; and, eventually, stimulating learning from the mistakes of others so as to be cognisant of unethical research practices.

Implementation in a School Scenario

How can this actually pan out inside a classroom?

Swartz (1976) has emphasised the need to take a leisurely look at mistakes without rushing to find solutions. He has argued that mistakes can be incorporated into a school's curriculum by exposing children to the notion that problem-solving is a dynamic phenomenon. He goes on to suggest ways of incorporating the scrutiny of mistakes into a school's curriculum. Much of what Swartz proposes is in alignment with the work described in this book. J. T. Bruer (1995) emphasised the need for teachers to explicitly teach simple strategies, such as how a student can read for understanding. Scott Paris and his colleagues ran a programme called the Informed Strategies of Learning (for details, see Mukunda 2009) where students' patterns of reading and their beliefs about it were worked with, so as to devise effective reading strategies.

While metacognitive skills have been shown by psychologists to develop naturally in some students, the work described here enabled students to *feel the need for these skills,* and then allowed an explicit training of students in this domain. In the course of the research work described in this book, students began to realise the gaps in the ways that they had been studying so far ('Oh, so *this* is how we should study!' exclaimed a student in one of the schools where this research was done), and then *sought out such remedial strategies* or devised them, with some help – *as and when they felt the need for them.*

Appropriateness for Indian Schools

The census data of 2011 shows that India's youth bulge is sharpest at the key 15-24 age group, even as its youngest and oldest age groups begin to narrow. Moreover, it shows that India's working age population is now 63.4 per cent of the total population (Gudaganavar and Gudaganavar 2014).

In a country with such a unique demographic advantage, it is self-evident that the fruits can be harvested only if the workforce is educated and well-equipped with the requisite skills. Thus, the criticality of autonomous learners cannot be overemphasised. It is impossible to ensure adequately trained teachers for each and every one of these young Indians; therefore, a metacognition of their own ways of learning and of erring is one way out. While teachers will always be needed to facilitate the learning of students, autonomous learners will emerge as the winners of the future. By empowering students to take charge of their own learning, this compilation envisions the emergence of reflective learners who enjoy the challenge that true learning usually is, unhindered by shame or diffidence in making mistakes along the way.

Growth Mindset

Stanford psychologist Carol S. Dweck (2006) has conducted pioneering work in the area of fixed and growth mindsets in her book *Mindset: The New Psychology of Success.* Her work brings out the power of our beliefs, and the remarkable impact of changing them even in a small way. A 'fixed mindset' is one which assumes that qualities like self-confidence, intelligence and motivation are inbuilt and cannot be changed in any significant way. A 'growth mindset', on the other hand, views failures as opportunities to stretch the capabilities of the mind and even to alter character. Simply by believing that intelligence and character can be changed, Dweck found that people (both children and adults) replace a hunger for approval with a passion for learning. While they certainly do not believe that everyone can be an Einstein or a Tagore, they do acknowledge that the true potential of a person is unknown, and therefore can be worked towards without being pulled back by imaginings of failure.

Moser et al. (2011) have actually gathered evidence for a neural mechanism for this growth mindset, and suggest that neural mechanisms indexing on-line awareness of (and attention to) mistakes are intimately involved in growth-minded individuals' ability to rebound from mistakes. It is therefore imperative that any sort of research which can generate the possibility of altering fixed mindsets (of learner as well as teacher) be supported and encouraged.

Seeing 'Missed Takes' in Mistakes

In a country like India, where performance in the examination is such an overwhelming criterion for assessing the worth of a candidate for any post, the significance of a growth mindset cannot be overemphasised. If only students were taught how to bounce back from a failure, acknowledge and learn from a mistake and admit to the potential of learning from another's mistake, none of this would happen. More often than not, students who give up (and in the worst case, commit suicide) are those who are convinced that they cannot make it – ever. Through a set of experiences that challenge this assumption, it is likely that a student's mindset can undergo a change.

This is an effort to regard mistakes as 'missed takes' – i.e. un-entered doorways that open into a learner's cognition of his/her own gaps in understanding, error patterns and unexplored avenues of application. This approach welcomes mistakes as opportunities rather than as pitfalls, and invites the learner to take a close look at the specific mistakes (s)he makes. By systematic scrutiny (through multiple frameworks that evolved through this study), it is envisioned that the learner will begin to regard the making of mistakes as natural, inevitable steps in the ladder of learning, and respect each one's unique pathway to the mastery of conceptual understanding, or even mere absorption of facts.

Action Research Framework

The Action Research (Lewin 1948) Framework of Plan-Act-Observe-Reflect (Costello 2011; Glanz 1999; Mills 2018) has been employed by the teacher-researchers in this study.[1] Since the motivation for undertaking this research sprang from a common need to address what was seen as a problem, the choice of *action research* as the most appropriate methodology is self-evident. If one teacher perceived the lack of motivation in a student as an issue, another saw the poor grasp of fundamentals as alarming. However, beyond this initial point, each teacher carved his/her own unique path. While all four teachers were aligned in the broad issue that they identified as their research problem (namely, enabling struggling students to feel empowered and stimulated by the subject), each one evolved their own plan according to their unique context. This is typical of action research, in that it allows an organic and unfettered exploration of likely ways of addressing the identified problem by each action researcher; and this is yet another reason why the method was deemed to be most suitable for these teacher-researchers.

Reflective Learner Programme

As mentioned in the Preface, a group of teacher educators at Thinking Teacher[2] designed an initiative called the Reflective Learner

---

[1] For a detailed description of the evolution of this framework and its applicability across disciplines, the reader is referred to Raghavan and Sood (2015).
[2] For details, see https://thinkingteacher.in.

Programme, with the intent of utilising the entry point of mistakes to draw out the reflective learners from students (and, as it turned out, in turn teachers). A half-day workshop to introduce the programme was first conducted for various teachers by the facilitator (also the compiler of this book), where the broad methodology of using mistakes as a doorway to understanding the minds of students was described. Thereafter, the option of engaging with the facilitator so as to actually carry out such action research was thrown open to *all* the teachers.

It is purely by chance that two English and two mathematics teachers chose to opt for this programme. Perhaps the choice was not entirely fortuitous. For decades, these two subjects have been the focus of attention for remedial classes in numerous Indian schools and homes. An untested surmise of this writer is that this could be due to the fact that one is either 'right' or 'wrong' in both these subjects. A study of the learning that lies behind examining the errors made in them, therefore, could – and did, as you will see – prove to be extremely beneficial to both the teacher and the taught.

Through periodic interactions with the facilitator, each teacher's action research was facilitated and systematically documented. The duration and frequency of these interactions varied for each of the teacher-researchers, and therefore, have been noted in each account differently. These engagements were online for schools whose geographical location did not permit regular visits, and face-to-face for those which lent themselves easily to this sort of engagement. While several strategies were arrived at by the researchers concerned (since they knew the context best), a few were occasionally suggested by the facilitator. Again, each teacher-researcher showed different degrees of independence, and this is also reflected in each account. The overall role of the facilitator was to nudge the teacher to think of multiple possibilities, enquire into an assumption, or gather convincing evidence of a perceived shift – and only occasionally, to suggest a strategy or two. As mentioned earlier, except in one case, documentation was carried out throughout the project in a non-formal manner by both the teacher-researcher as well as the facilitator, and the entire body of work was put together, in the form that you now see, at the end of each teacher's research. It was during the final stage of documentation that the facilitator played the most significant role.

Within this broad framework of Plan-Act-Observe-Reflect, therefore, this book offers a variety of ways for a teacher-researcher to engage with the problem of turning mistakes into 'missed takes'. It is hoped that these authentic case studies will convince the reader not only of the rich rewards of such an exercise but also of its feasibility. Before launching into this sort of work, the estimated investment of time and effort often puts off the potential beneficiary of the programme. It is the earnest request of this writer that the decision (not) to undertake such an effort be put on hold – until this entire book is read through. The voices of teachers and students who participated in the programme are the best sources for such a cross-check.

References

Bruer, J. T. 1995. *Schools for Thought.* Cambridge: MIT Press.

Chalmers, A. F. 1973. 'On Learning from Our Mistakes'. *The British Journal for the Philosophy of Science* 24(2): 164-173.

Costello, Patrick J. M. 2011. *Effective Action Research: Developing Reflective Thinking and Practice.* 2nd Ed. New York: Continuum.

Dweck, C. S. 2006. *Mindset: The New Psychology of Success.* New York: Random House.

Gangola, A., J. Kathait, S. Rai, R. Sharma, S. Semwal, A. Bisht, V. Chauhan, K. Kandpal, S. Shah, K. Joshi, E. Sharma and A. Chomal. 2011(a). 'Assessment Reform and Sustainable Change in Education Part I'. In *Proceedings of epiSTEME 4 – International Conference to Review Research on Science, Technology and Mathematics Education,* edited by S. Chunawala and M. Kharatmal, pp. 217-223. India:

Macmillan. http://episteme4.hbcse.tifr.res.in/proceedings/strand-iii-curriculum-and-pedagogical-studies-in-stme/gangola-1.

———. 2011(b). 'Assessment Reform and Sustainable Change in Education Part II'. In *Proceedings of epiSTEME 4 – International Conference to Review Research on Science, Technology and Mathematics Education*, edited by S. Chunawala and M. Kharatmal, pp. 225-231. India: Macmillan. http://episteme4.hbcse.tifr.res.in/proceedings/strand-iii-curriculum-and-pedagogical-studies-in-stme/gangola-2.

Gibelman, M., and S. R. Gelman. 2001. 'Learning from the Mistakes of Others: A Look at Scientific Misconduct in Research'. *Journal of Social Work Education* 37(2): 241–254.

Glanz, Jeffrey. May–June 1999. 'A Primer on Action Research for the School Administrator'. *The Clearing House* 72(5): 301–304.

Gudaganavar, Nagaraj V., and Rajashri S. Gudaganavar. 2014. 'Demographic Dividend – Its Implications to India'. *Paripex: Indian Journal of Research* 3(1): 46-50.

Lewin, K. 1948. 'Action Research and Minority Problems'. In *Resolving Social Conflicts*, edited by G. W. Lewin. New York: Harper & Row.

Locklin, B. S. 2013. 'Learning from Our Mistakes: Difficulty and Insight in the Literature Classroom'. *The Journal of the Midwest Modern Language Association* 46(1): 55-69.

Mills, G. E. 2018. *Action Research: A Guide for the Teacher Researcher.* New Jersey: Pearson Merrill Prentice Hall.

Moser, J. S., H. S. Schroder, C. Heeter, T. O. Moran and Y. H. Lee. 2011. 'Mind Your Errors: Evidence for a Neural Mechanism Linking Growth Mind-Set to Adaptive Post-error Adjustments'. *Psychological Science* 22(12): 1484-1489.

Mukunda, Kamala V. 2009. *What Did You Ask at School Today? A Handbook of Child Learning.* New Delhi: Harper Collins.

Popper, Karl R. 1962. *Conjectures and Refutations: The Growth of Scientific Knowledge.* New York: Basic Books.

Raghavan, N., and V. Sood. 2015. *The Reflective Teacher.* Chennai: Orient Blackswan.

Sconyers, J. 1976. 'The Theorem that Wasn't, or, Learning from a Mistake'. *Mathematics in School* 5(5): 30.

Swartz, R. 1976. 'Mistakes as an Important Part of the Learning Process'. *The High School Journal* 59(6): 246-257.

ERRING TO LEARN

What can a teacher do to instil confidence in young children so that they read, write and engage in class without the fear of making mistakes? If answers can be found to this question – throwing open an array of strategies for the interested teacher – surely the familiar problem of inadequate communication skills in English can be nipped in the bud? It is perhaps worth reflecting here that conventional strategies which are commonly adopted to 'improve student performance' (e.g. reducing marks, withdrawing privileges or rewarding the best performers) seldom serve to address the fear that lies within the one who is committing the mistake; and therefore, none have a lasting impact.

This is an account of a fifth-grade teacher of English and social studies who undertook an action research study to answer this very question. Within a short period of time, she achieved remarkable results. Her trajectory over a period of about four months and her own reflections are summarised in this chapter.

The Teacher-Researcher

At the time of conducting this research, Prerna Pradhan was teaching English and social studies to Grade V in Taktse International School, Sikkim. For quite some time, Prerna had been concerned with the lack of visible signs of learning in a few students, and had been making unsuccessful attempts to understand these children. For example, she perceived one student donning a blasé 'I don't care' mask, and mistakenly interpreted it as her enjoying a certain impunity as the daughter of an influential person. She noticed that certain others needed to be repeatedly told to take care of their belongings or note down the day's homework. Therefore, she was looking for ways of tackling such issues when the option of joining the Reflective Learner Programme was given to her.

She joined the Reflective Learner Programme in the third week of July 2016 with the intent of helping a few 'struggling students'. Over the next few months, Prerna focused on language development particularly for these students – including the rest of the class as and when she deemed fit – while teaching both English and social studies, and devised common strategies for

Dear Akka:

I have started with spelling and proofreading. For Anita, I gave her work to complete a story and motivated her. I am sending her to Grade 2, to do read aloud for the juniors – she seemed excited. In my next mail, I will write about how it's going and what we need to talk about.

– Prerna's email to the facilitator

both subjects. At the end of the programme, she had not only empowered students to take the onus for their own growth, but also challenged her own assumptions (as a teacher) about students' mindsets.

Systemic Demand from the School

In Taktse International School, there is a well-established practice of students, across grades, proofreading their work before submitting it to the teacher (they mark their errors in green ink, so that it is noticeable; and at the end of the exercise, write 'proofread', again, in green). Thus, there is a

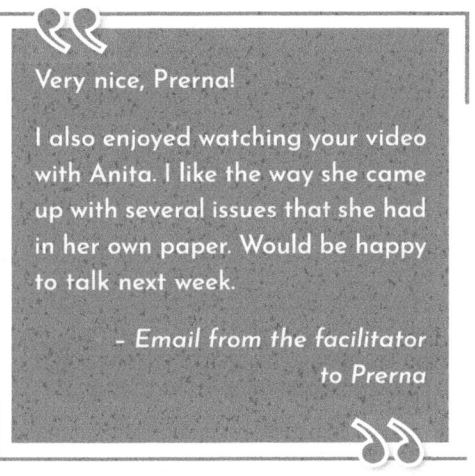

Very nice, Prerna!

I also enjoyed watching your video with Anita. I like the way she came up with several issues that she had in her own paper. Would be happy to talk next week.

- Email from the facilitator to Prerna

systemic demand (from the school) on students to go through their work carefully before turning it in. Prerna, too, followed this practice.

Timeline

Prerna participated in the Reflective Learner Programme from the third week of July until early December 2016. At the end of this period, she drew up a timeline (see Table 1) to understand how many actual working days had been available for the task. (In October, several festival-related holidays had prevented her from devoting adequate time.) As can be seen from Table 1, the entire action research was conducted by Prerna in less than four months, without accounting for the initial two-week warm-up period in July.

Table 1: Prerna's timeline

Months	August	September	October	November	December
Dates	1-5	1-2	3-6	1-4	1-2
	8-12	5-9	Pooja break	7-11	
	15-19	12-16	17-21	14-18	
	22-26	19-23	24-28	21-25	
	29-31	26-30	31	27-30	

Sample under Study

Prerna identified three struggling students in Grade V as her sample for the study. Her basis for this selection were the visible signs of inability to cope that each of these children showed. She spoke to the facilitator of how these students[1] – Abhinav, Priya and Anita – seemed to be struggling in class. All of them had trouble proofreading their work; in addition, they had a range of difficulties from spellings to grammar. For example, Abhinav had a severe issue with time management – from going out late for recess to submitting his assignments late. On the facilitator's prompting, Prerna made a detailed compilation of their struggles at the start of her research (see Table 2).

Table 2: Initial location of the three students that Prerna chose to work with

S. no.	Name of student	Issues
1	Abhinav	• Unable to spot his own errors • Unable to form clear sentences • Makes careless spelling mistakes • Copies incorrect spellings from questions • Makes capitalisation errors (concept taught in the class) • Makes many punctuation errors in written work

---

[1] All names have been changed to preserve confidentiality.

2	Priya	• Unable to understand any given passage • Answers whatever she wants • Unable to understand questions • Does not proofread her work • Makes too many spelling mistakes • Makes many grammatical errors (verb constancy, run-on sentences, present-past-future all together) • Repeats words (e.g. he *told told* me) • Unable to see that her answers are not connected to the topic • Unable to apply the concept taught in the class • Writes in a haphazard manner
3	Anita	• Makes capitalisation errors • Unable to form proper sentences • Unable to see that her answers are not connected to the topic • Does not make sense of what she is writing • Does not understand questions at all • Makes spelling mistakes • Makes many grammatical mistakes • Answers verbally but while writing, writes little or nothing • Makes punctuation errors • Writes only simple sentences – not up to her grade expectation • Takes a long time to complete her work, but writes very little

Here, it needs to be pointed out that Prerna did not ever take these three students separately out of class. Therefore, while her strategies were often directed to the entire class, (as it often benefited many of them) she made particular note of how these three children were coping. In other words, she systematically gathered data only about these three students so as to monitor their progress.

Teacher-Facilitator Engagement

From the last week of July to the end of November 2016, there were about eight teacher-facilitator interactions over Skype or WhatsApp – about two to three times a month. During these sessions, Prerna shared her issues, and then she and the facilitator together agreed upon certain strategies that could be implemented. These strategies were sometimes for the entire class, and at other times, only for the three 'struggling' students. Thus, depending upon the context and the current concerns, Prerna adapted the strategies to suit her needs; and on certain occasions, she even devised her own strategies without the help of the facilitator.

Preparing the Ground

Prerna drew up a timetable for the three already identified students of Grade V immediately after joining the Reflective Learner Programme. The idea was to systematically focus on individual students' errors across the period of her action research (see Table 3).

Table 3: Plan for students

Week	Abhinav	Priya	Anita
August 8-12	Time management	Reading	Reading; participating in read-aloud activity
Aug. 15-Sep. 2	Spelling	Spelling	Spelling
Aug. 5-Sep. 9	Reading instructions carefully	Reading questions	Writing clear sentences
Sep. 12-19	Reading a question plus looking at the marks for that question	Learning to pronounce words with multiple syllables	Writing and proofreading for comma, full stop and question mark
Oct. 23-Dec. 6	Proofreading for comma, full stop and question mark	Reading and guessing the meaning	Reading instructions carefully; submitting work on time

However, she soon found that she was not able to follow the timetable because the palpable fears in her students were preventing her from moving ahead. Prerna quickly realised the need to let go of the timetable and instead invest her time and energy in squarely addressing her students' fears – and, in so doing, she simply responded organically to the actual situation.

For this purpose, in August and September, Prerna made detailed observations about the behaviour and significant characteristics of the students in Grade V, in addition to the mistakes made by them. Sensing their fear of making mistakes and of the teacher, Prerna spent considerable time increasing their levels of comfort in *first sharing their mistakes with her*. She knew that she could not suddenly drop the role of a teacher and don that of their 'buddy', and that she had to strike a balance between these two roles. She was also aware that she would have to acknowledge the efforts of the 'struggling' students without singling them out; and importantly, she could not be seen as neglecting the other students vis-à-vis these three.

Having made the effort to know all her students, she first shared with the class her positive observations about each one, in combination with the 'struggling' three. For instance, Prerna appreciated Anita as well as another student for their reading habits, and asked them to suggest books for the rest of the class to read. Similarly, Prerna appreciated both Abhinav and another student for their skill in solving the Rubik's Cube, and organised a match between the two. Abhinav's competitor won this match, but playing a match with a fellow student helped draw out the shy Abhinav, who slowly began opening up to Prerna. Thus, while acknowledging the efforts of Anita and Abhinav and praising them (to enhance their self-confidence), she also ensured that the class did not view her as being focused solely on a specific student.

Such efforts slowly helped develop a new level of comfort between Prerna and the students. Consequently, the fear-free environment allowed her to work on their mistakes swiftly, and she completed the programme in less than three months.

Prerna saw the need to address this ubiquitous fear, and her results (as described later) are self-evident. By engaging with her students both as an entire class, as well as on a one-on-one basis, she systematically tackled their attitudinal blocks before bringing out their mistakes for discussion. In so doing, even something as common as carelessness got addressed.

Whole-Class Strategies

In alignment with her intent to include all the students in her efforts, even as she conducted action research on just the three struggling students, Prerna decided to begin with something that would draw in the entire class.

It so panned out that on the day of the trial, Prerna was scheduled to show them their corrected answer scripts, always a tricky event. Therefore, to turn this formidable event into a casual exercise, she initiated a discussion by asking them questions like *why* did they feel they had scored low marks, or why did they think that no student scored full marks. In response, the students seemed aware that this was *because of their mistakes* – however, they were not sure of the *kinds of mistakes*.

Flip chart to list out common errors

In consultation with the facilitator, she arrived at a whole-class approach that would enable the students to identify the common mistakes of all the fifth graders. For this purpose, Prerna made a chart of common errors (listing mistakes of each and every student in the class, without naming them) and then discussed it with the whole class in a non-judgemental manner.

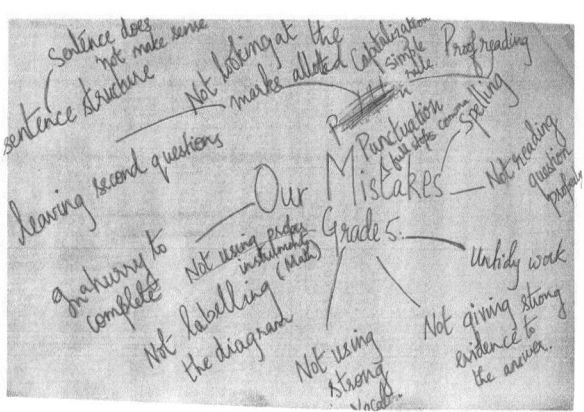

Figure 1: Commonly made mistakes

So, Prerna and the class together decided to list out their *commonly made mistakes*. As the students called out their typical errors, one by one, she began writing them on the flip chart. Almost all the students admitted to commonly made mistakes such as spelling and punctuation errors, not proofreading their work, not reading and answering the questions properly, leaving the second part of questions unanswered, not looking at the marks allotted to each question (and thus answering accordingly), not drawing inferences and not understanding the questions or passages (see Figure 1).

Prerna noticed that the three 'struggling' students also slowly began acknowledging their own errors. (Whenever she noticed that certain specific errors made by them were missing, she called those out, which then drew out the acknowledgement from these students, too.)

Once this exercise was over, Prerna distributed the corrected scripts. In her experience, the distribution of corrected answer scripts always resulted in a chaotic situation in class: students' numerous comparisons with their peers, clarifications and requests for more marks, etc. Therefore, on this occasion, she decided to tackle this issue by setting clear expectations right at the outset. She began by telling the students about the mistakes that *she* made (e.g. mispronouncing words), and even confided in them that she was learning as she went along, stressing on her will to improve. She finally asked them, 'How about you? Do *you* want to improve?'

When she received a resounding 'Yes!' from her bunch of fifth graders, she emphasised that while they would now collectively embark on an effort to improve, there was just one condition:

> We will not compare our work with each other. We will just identify *our own mistakes* so that we can try and make fewer mistakes in the next exercise. Let us see who is honest – can we all be honest? Let us see how many mistakes we can identify on our own. There is absolutely no need to feel ashamed …

Once the atmosphere was sombre enough, Prerna handed out the corrected answer scripts. As the students started comparing their answer scripts with the mistakes displayed on the flip chart (prepared earlier), they could now identify more mistakes.

She then went a step further by drawing their attention to the marks allotted for each question and the consequent loss of marks if an error was made. She asked them, 'What do you think a two-mark question demands in the answer?' They thought and declared that a two-mark answer should be three lines long, while a five-mark answer should be six to seven lines long. Prerna accepted these responses – all she wanted was to bring this parameter (alignment between answers and allotted marks) into their field of awareness.

Prerna realised that this entire exercise had worked: even the 'struggling' students (who had formerly not been aware of their errors) were able to identify their own mistakes – just by looking at the flip chart.

Memory game for spellings

A second strategy that Prerna decided to use for the benefit of the entire class was a memory game for enhancing the spelling skills of all the fifth graders. She wrote a variety of multisyllabic words on the flip chart (see Figure 2), and asked the entire class to look at them carefully for a few moments. After counting 1 through 10, she covered the chart, and asked them to write in their notebooks as many words as they could recall.

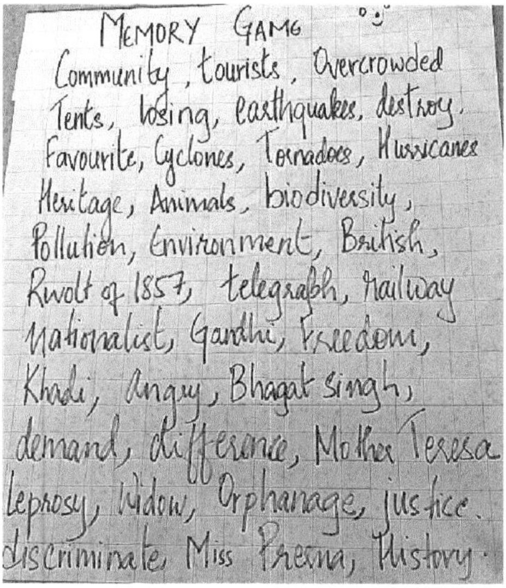

Figure 2: Learning to spell via a memory game

At first, the class displayed no interest at all. Noticing this, Prerna realised that there was a need to modify the game. So, in the next class, she announced an incentive:

'Whoever can memorise the maximum number of words, can read aloud from our book for an extra five minutes.' (All her fifth graders love to read texts aloud in class and it is deemed a privilege.) This spiked their interest, and they took part more animatedly. On the next run of the game, she changed the privilege to being allowed to complete the homework in class – during the last block[2]. Thus, she kept changing the incentive: sometimes, giving chocolates, sometimes allowing the winner to go out and read a book of their choice and so on. Further, Prerna was aware that expecting them to recall *all* the words was unrealistic. So, she selected those who could remember 30, 31 or 32 words, called them to her desk, checked their spellings and allowed them the incentive for the day.

Moreover, since the students seemed to really enjoy the memory game for spellings, Prerna conducted it every day (changing most of the words, while retaining a few).

The recreation aspect notwithstanding, Prerna added another dimension to this game. Once a week, she asked all the students, without exclusion, to make their own spelling lists comprising commonly made mistakes by them. Since she could not check all the lists individually, she asked each student to pair up (each had to select a 'buddy', and hand over their list to this buddy). The buddies in each pair took turns to dictate words from the other's spelling list, and the one who was not dictating had to write them down correctly. Then the buddies were required to check each other's spellings. In addition, during weekends, all the students were advised to master the incorrect spellings from their own lists. The creation of individual spelling lists helped them to overcome their areas of difficulty. Slowly, the number of errors decreased for every student. (Prerna fine-tuned this strategy without any inputs from the facilitator – just based on her instincts.)

By November, the entire class was able to recall the spellings of most words correctly (as a reward, the entire class chose to go out for a walk with their teacher). For this bunch of fifth graders, learning

---

[2] A block is an extended period, e.g. two 40-minute periods clubbed together.

to spell correctly became easy – and fun. Prerna deemed the game to master spellings a huge success because the students were focused and eager to memorise more words with each round. Not only did the game help in improving their spellings to a great extent, it also turned into a very popular activity in class.

Strategies to Address Issues Faced by the Three Struggling Students

At the start, strategies to address concerns were jointly arrived at by the facilitator and Prerna through discussion. For instance, when Prerna lamented Abhinav's need to be repeatedly reminded about the simplest of tasks, the facilitator noted that this could be indicative of a lack of focus on the part of the child. So, she suggested the following two versions of a memory game to heighten Abhinav's focus:

✦ The teacher shows a set of just 5 to 10 words to the students for a few minutes, and then removes the display. Then, within one minute, the students are asked to write as many words as they can remember from this set (how she then built on this strategy is discussed later).

✦ The teacher shows images of 10 different items to the students for less than a minute, and then removes them from the field of vision. Finally, the students are asked to recall as many images as they can from this set.

When it came to Priya, the teacher noted that this child comprehended well during benchmark assessments and guided reading; however, she struggled to comprehend while reading *on her own*. Prerna observed that Priya seemed to struggle with reading long words, and needed to break them up into parts. The facilitator pointed out that this was probably because *that was how Priya was seeing the words*: in bits and bytes. The strategy suggested for Priya included covering each word partially as she read – slowly, uncovering that word bit by bit; so that, later on, she could follow the same process *in her own mind*.

Prerna first asked Priya to cover *known words*, and found that she was able to pronounce them. The teacher then extended the strategy to *unknown words* as well. This was done in two steps:

Step 1. Covering the unknown portion – so as to first reveal a familiar portion of the word.

Step 2. Covering the familiar part of the word, thus challenging Priya *to first decipher the unfamiliar part.*

Within three to four weeks of practising thus, Priya began to read with greater confidence and pronounced words correctly, without fumbling.

Anita had been struggling in class since Grade I, when she first joined the school. Prerna shared with the facilitator that Anita acted as if she enjoyed a certain impunity and donned an 'I don't care' mask – or perhaps, *truly* did not care. She also seemed to be able to answer questions *orally* – but never in writing. No matter how hard Prerna tried to draw her out, Anita did not seem to put in the effort. When Prerna tried counselling her, she did indeed show some receptivity, but the impact lasted all of two days. The facilitator noted that this could be indicative of low self confidence in the child, coupled with some *pretence of indifference.* So, an appropriate question that immediately arose was: What did Anita *like to do*? Anita liked to read, so a few strategies were suggested that could make use of her love for reading. Moreover, since the current premise was based on building Anita's self-confidence first, Prerna could begin by frequently acknowledging and appreciating Anita's efforts (howsoever minimal). She could then take advantage of Anita's love for reading by telling her to take on one or more of the following tasks:

1. *Completing an unfinished story* – Prerna tried this out, and found that after completing just one unfinished story, Anita expressed the desire to write her own stories.

2. *Playing the role of quizmaster* – This was done as a class activity, where Prerna divided the class into two groups, and the members of each group were to take turns and ask questions. Naturally, Anita, too, participated. Prerna found that focusing on the entire class helped, as Anita did not feel singled out.

3. *Making question papers* – This, too was a class activity. After completing a chapter, Prerna gave students the option of choosing their own 'buddy'. Each pair was then supposed to create two questions from the chapter, after which they had to share their questions with the whole class (to make it more interesting, they could even answer their own questions, after allowing others to try).

4. *Writing a story for reading aloud* – Anita was asked to write a story, and then read it aloud to Grade II. The idea behind this strategy was that since she loved reading aloud, it would motivate her to write, which was where she experienced difficulty. She did indeed get inspired to write. Thus, this helped her view writing as *a means to a desirable end* (reading aloud to Grade II), instead of *an end in itself.*

Prerna now began to diligently focus on her three 'struggling' students and systematically tackled each of their errors with a variety of strategies.

Abhinav

Prerna first decided to tackle Abhinav's difficulty in spelling words. She began by observing Abhinav's pronunciation of words, in order to check whether or not his spelling errors were due to incorrect pronunciation. She found that his pronunciations were correct but the spellings were not; so, she asked him to include these misspelt words to his spelling list. He paid heed to her suggestion, and made a list of words he found difficult to spell (he even posted it in his dorm for regular access).

The critical point in the above observation is that the student was empowered to *make his own list of words that he found difficult to spell.* This act allowed Prerna to *shift the onus of spotting an area of learning difficulty* from the teacher to the learner. It required Abhinav *to step back and examine where his difficulty lay.* Thereafter, the student felt motivated to set himself the target of mastering the spellings of a certain number of words. By the end of October, Abhinav could spell over 50 per cent of these words correctly.

Figures 3 and 4 illustrate two samples of Abhinav's work, work done at the start and towards the end of the Reflective Learner Programme, respectively.

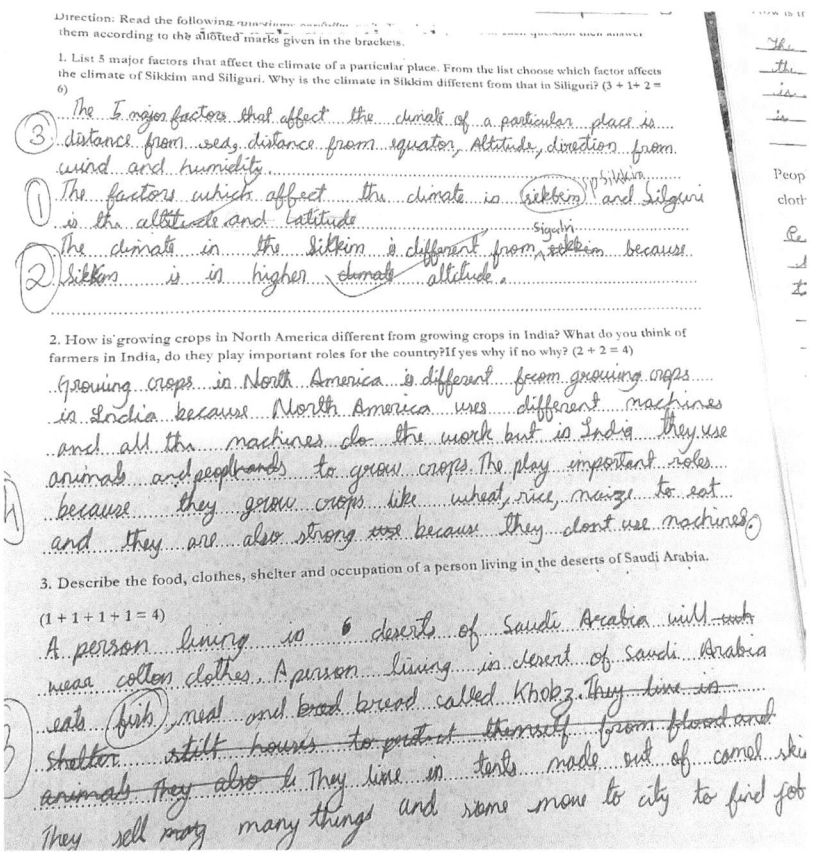

Figure 3: Abhinav's work at the start of the programme

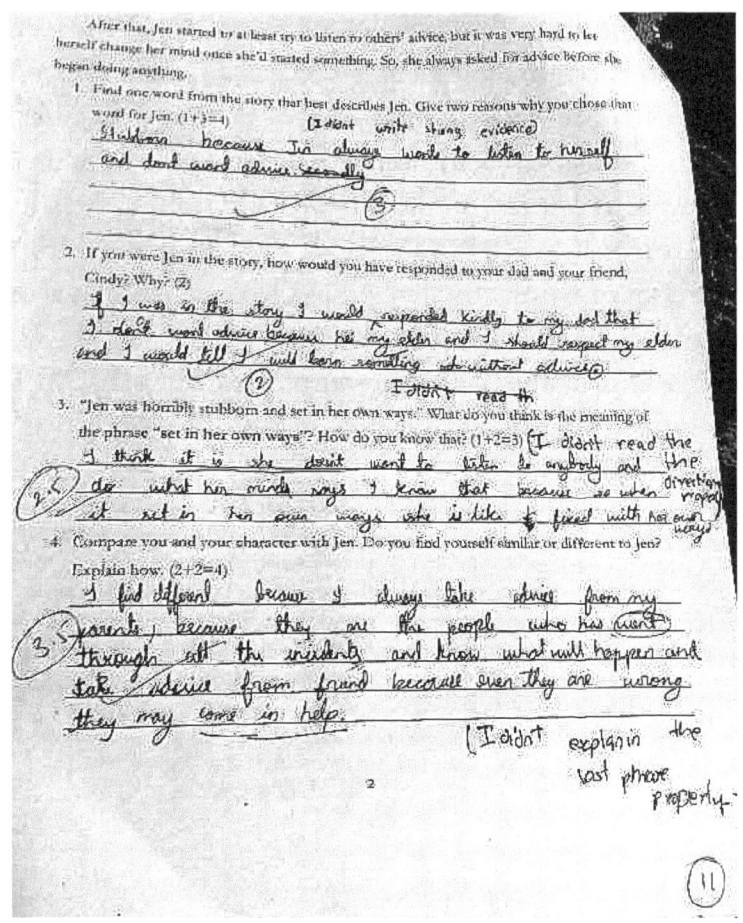

Figure 4: Abhinav's work towards the end of the programme

Figure 4 shows Abhinav making acknowledgements like 'I didn't write strong evidence'; 'I didn't read the directions properly'; and 'I didn't explain the last phrase properly'. These are indicators of enhanced self-awareness in the student. In addition, it shows *no spelling errors at all!*

Next, Prerna attempted to address his time management skills. For this purpose, she made use of Abhinav's skill in solving the Rubik's Cube. (Some years earlier, the Taktse International School Principal had introduced the Rubik's Cube in all classes as a tool to help sharpen the cognitive skills of students in a playful manner.) As Prerna often saw Abhinav (and many others) playing with it during free time, she decided to take advantage of their interest. Before each class began, she would ask the fifth graders to arrange the Rubik's Cube correctly. To her surprise, Abhinav was *always* the first to finish this particular task – at worst, second! Quick to spot an opportunity, she told him appreciatively: 'You are a *really quick* boy! Can you do the same with submitting your work on time, packing and unpacking bags, etc.?' This acknowledgement from his teacher seemed to have had an impact on him, and Abhinav's time management skills improved rapidly: so much so that by the end of the Reflective Learner Programme, there was *absolutely no such issue.*

By the third month, Prerna noted that Abhinav was *able to spot the mistakes, but was not yet ready to correct them*; so, she decided to introduce strategies for tackling this difficulty. Amongst the strategies she employed was a punctuation game (suggested by the facilitator). The game involved changing the intonation as one read aloud, suggesting the need for a certain punctuation at each inflexion. For instance, raising the voice in enquiry called for the insertion of a question mark, bringing in excitement pointed out the need for an exclamation mark, pausing a short while for a comma and pausing longer for a full stop. (Once she saw that Abhinav was comfortable enough with the game, Prerna decided to introduce it in the class as well. Reading the words in a certain tone helped them understand which punctuation would be correct at a particular point in a text; they also learnt to read with expression through this. The teacher also ensured that each one of them got a chance to read.)

Further, in Taktse, all classes have a 'read along book' – where the teacher is supposed to read along with the class, with expression. Prerna utilised this feature by giving chances to a different student each day – not only to Abhinav. When Abhinav's turn came, his use of punctuation in reading was appreciated. What really helped was praising him with specifics, not just saying, 'Good job, Abhinav', but holding up his work and then saying: 'Abhinav, I notice that your sentences are clear and you have used complex sentences!'

At the end of this exercise, she noted that Abhinav could understand sentences from a given text; however, he still wrote sentences that were not clear or were grammatically incorrect. Nonetheless, there was some progress, too, as she observed that his spoken skills were better: even though he spoke fast, he did not now mix genders or tenses, and was also a good reader. She also noted that though Abhinav had initially faced problems with capitalisation, he was now showing signs of improvement. He was already good at pausing for punctuations when reading a text, and now, after special lessons on punctuation in writing, he was getting better at punctuating his written work correctly, too.

Priya

Given the numerous issues that Priya was facing (see Table 2), Prerna first decided to sort out the lack of clarity in Priya's work. (Figure 5 highlights some of the lacunae in Priya's work.) Her answers often did not make sense, and Prerna felt that it was because Priya did not read questions with care.

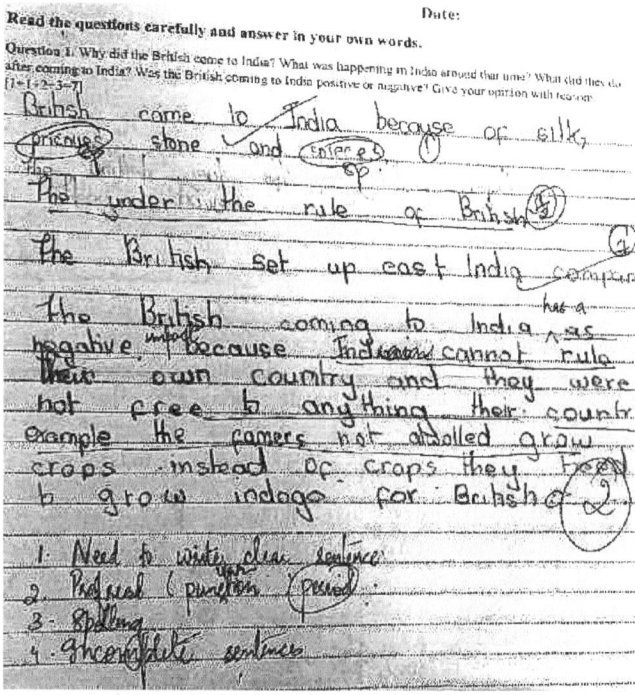

Figure 5: Sample of Priya's work

Prerna decided to tackle this challenge in the following manner: She organised silent reading sessions for all the students in Grade V during the school's weekly period titled DEAR (Drop Everything and Read) – on Mondays. During this period, the entire school literally dropped everything and read, including teachers and administrative staff.

In order to help the slow readers feel supported, the teacher gave them the option of choosing a reading buddy. (Of course, not all the children needed a reading buddy – only about 10 children in the class were paired up.) Priya chose a 'reading buddy', and so did Prerna – as an indication to the class that even teachers may need to improve their reading skills. (Strategically, Prerna chose as her reading buddies those who hardly read; and she also kept changing them after reading one book with each.)

Further, in all English and social studies classes, students of Taktse International are expected to read a 'pleasure reading book' for 10 minutes. So Prerna utilised those moments as well for nudging the reader in Priya. She would often ask Priya about the book she was reading presently, the challenges she was facing and so on. Sometimes she would read together with Priya, too, particularly when all others were busy with their classwork. Hand-holding her in this manner, Prerna kept encouraging her.

Prerna noted that Priya read a number of books in 2016 – the year that this research was conducted – whereas formerly she would hardly ever read. She also appreciated that Priya was not afraid of making mistakes while either reading aloud or talking; and even acknowledged this trait of hers before the entire class, saying that Priya was able to carry on undeterred even if her friends made fun of her – and that this rare quality of hers would really take her forward. This further boosted Priya's morale.

It is important to highlight here that the student (Priya) was making mistakes freely, though *she was not yet aware that they were mistakes*. Her lack of inhibition in attempting to read aloud or answer, even if she was not sure of being right, was appreciated by the teacher. Another noteworthy point in the teacher's journey, too, was Prerna's attitude to this student that reveals her own open mindset towards mistakes: an admiration of one who can freely make mistakes and acknowledge them. Moreover, Prerna went a step further and drew the attention of the entire class to such a remarkable trait – and in so doing, pulled them, too, towards such behaviour! It now remained for Priya to move to the next step: i.e. seeing how to correct the mistake *after it has been seen to be one.*

By the third month of the programme, Priya was sensitised *to see where she had made a mistake* and acknowledge it. Figures 6(a) and (b) illustrate samples of Priya's work during this time period. In Figure 6(a), Priya writes, self-questioningly: 'I have not done the second part of the question: Why?' Again, in Figure 6(b), she candidly admits: 'I did not understand the question and got confused.' She also notes where she was correct by stating simply: 'This is correct.'

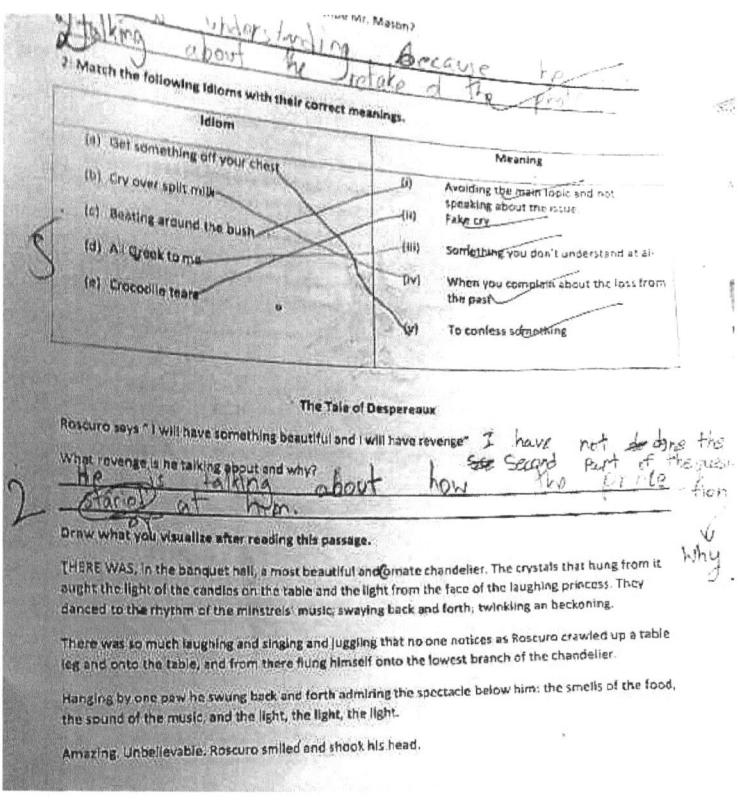

(a)

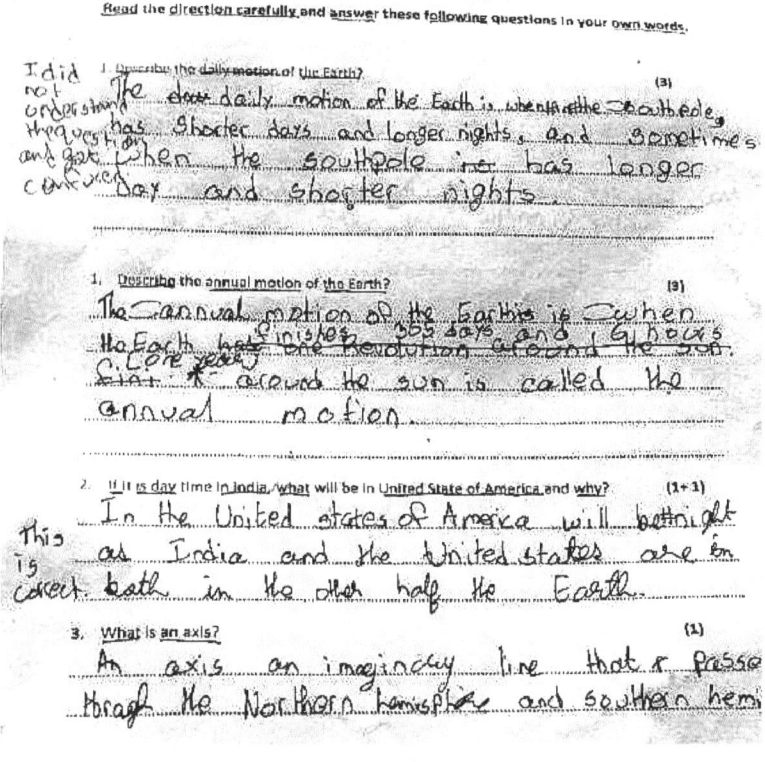

(b)

Figure 6: Samples of Priya's work indicating (a) self-questioning and (b) self-confidence

Thus, Priya slowly became aware of her repeated tendency to read a question without sufficient attention, and consequently answer it incorrectly.

The next challenge that Prerna tackled was developing Priya's sentence structure. She told Priya to look at her work and rewrite it over and over again. This was done as part of the routine classwork. Thus, there was absolutely no need to take time out for conducting extra classes just for Priya.

In order to tackle Priya's spelling errors, the facilitator suggested the following strategy to Prerna:

Give Priya 10 spellings. Ask her to write them on a Post-it note and stick it on her bathroom mirror. Then ask her to challenge herself to recall these spellings daily – and once she is done, she can come for a test, when you can check her progress.

Prerna found that this strategy worked, too. In this way, over the period of this study, Prerna successfully tackled each of Priya's issues one by one.

Anita

Here was a case of the teacher-researcher revising her stand on a student, after receiving a different perspective from the facilitator. When Prerna shared her suspicion with the facilitator that Anita seemed to be indifferent as she probably thought she enjoyed a certain impunity (being the daughter of an influential person) the facilitator drew out more of Prerna's observations about the child. As Prerna described the child's behaviour, the facilitator questioned the notion that the child was indifferent or blasé. Instead, she observed that the child's behaviour was reeking of a lack of self-confidence. With openness, Prerna immediately showed her willingness to explore this possibility.

Prerna attempted to work on Anita's possible lack of self-confidence by asking her to participate in a read-aloud session for Grade II. Within two weeks, Anita began showing signs of progress: she had started participating in the assemblies, as well as in the class. Anita even approached Prerna for more read-aloud sessions in other grades. Anita's progress confirmed to both Prerna and the facilitator that this was indeed a problem of lack of self-confidence, not one of arrogance. No sooner was the issue of self-confidence addressed than Anita started opening up.

As Anita's confidence increased, she also became increasingly self-aware in her work, and started noting her own errors, as shown in Figure 7.

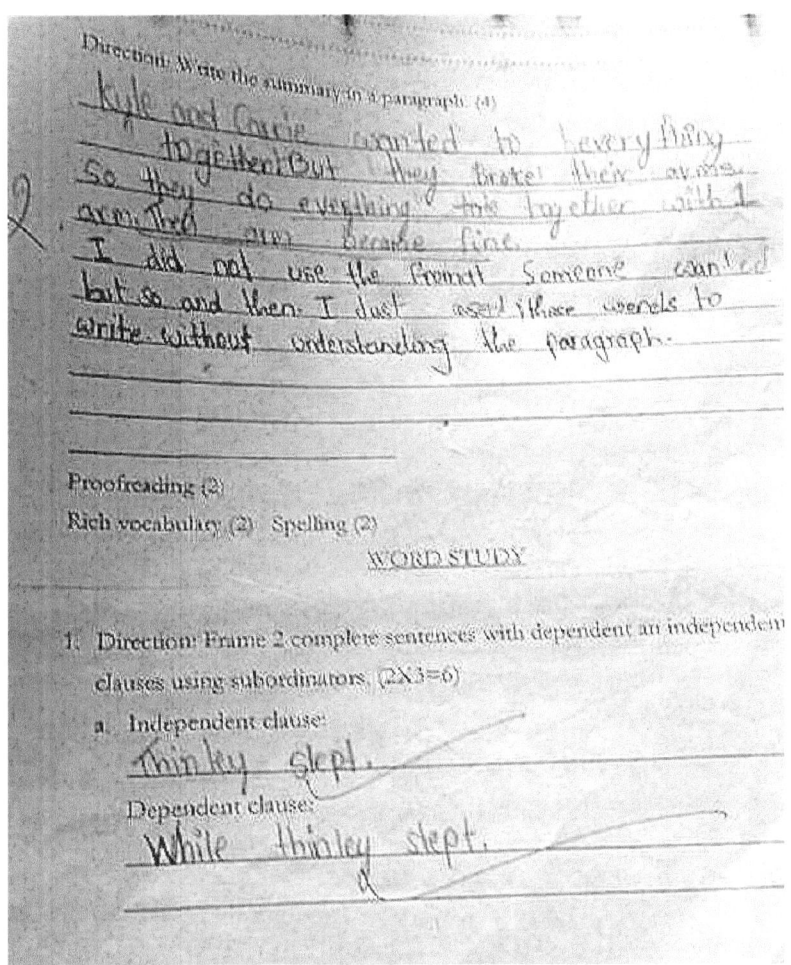

Figure 7: Sample of Anita's work indicating awareness about her own errors

That such a reflection bore fruit is also evident from a narrative that Anita wrote in September 2016 (see Figure 8).

However, it took time for such a change to manifest in a sustained manner, as there were many frustrating moments when Anita appeared to slip back into a 'don't care' mode. Prerna was a little perplexed about this tendency of hers, and shared it with the facilitator. She was relieved when the facilitator drew her attention to the positive feedback about Anita from other teachers: all of whom confirmed noticeable improvement in Anita (see Figure 9).

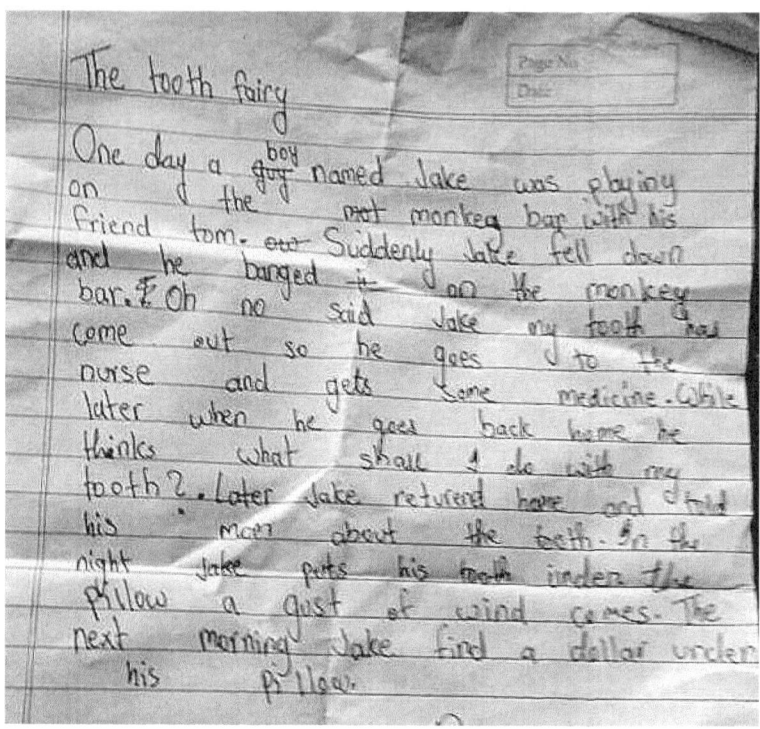

Figure 8: A story written by Anita

Anita has started to submit her work on time. She completes her work, but she needs to proofread more carefully. — *Science Teacher*	She is progressing and is regular with her work. — *Math Teacher*	Anita's reading ability in Hindi has improved, and she can recognise Hindi alphabet. — *Hindi Teacher*

Figure 9: Teachers' feedback on Anita's progress

Happy with Anita's progress, Prerna recollected that earlier she used to consider Anita a lazy child, and that *the child knew it*. However, even though she no longer felt the same, she realised that the child still needed constant monitoring and pushing. She was ultimately satisfied that her coaxing had helped Anita come out of her shell. There is a very powerful realisation embedded in Prerna's admission here: that *whatever the teacher felt about the child was being felt silently by the child, too, who responded in kind each time.* It is remarkable that Prerna came to clearly see how her earlier premise (whether true or false) had affected the student, as well as how her altered premise had also affected her.

Developing Self-Evaluation Skills in Students

In the third month, the facilitator suggested to Prerna the strategy of not marking the mistakes on the paper, but to give the corrected sheets to the students and ask them to identify their own mistakes. When Prerna tried out this strategy, she found that several students could only identify spelling and punctuation errors – but when they misunderstood a question, they could not identify the source of the problem. Prerna admitted that this was a new learning for her.

> Thank you for your support, and for helping me grow as a thinking teacher.
>
> I had started feeling that I was old to learn things, but when I saw you and other Akkas in my school, I realised that learning never ends. You have inspired me a lot!
>
> – Prerna's email to the facilitator

Among the three struggling students, Abhinav and Priya showed good progress in the area of self-evaluation. Anita reached the stage of being able to identify all her spelling mistakes, even though she did not learn to write correctly.

As Abhinav's enhanced ability to identify his own spelling errors has already been discussed earlier, this section focuses on Priya's progress.

Priya's evaluation (and self-evaluation) skills came to light after the facilitator made the following suggestion to Prerna: 'Let Priya check another student's work, and subsequently, ask her to proofread her own.' (Prerna implemented this strategy primarily in order to make Priya cognisant of the alignment between marks allotted to a question and the length of its answer.)

Prerna asked Priya to play 'teacher' for a day and correct the work of a student of her choice. Without hesitation, Priya

> ❝ But you were *always* a thinking teacher, Prerna! I did not have to turn you into one. If you were not so, how could you have been so concerned about your students' lack of motivation? How often you shared with me your worries: a teacher who is not a thinking teacher has no such worries! It was so nice to see the manner in which you implemented the suggestions. I am sure I will get to know more about your efforts once you get down to documenting them in detail. Please do so before you forget your wonderful efforts: anyone can forget as time elapses.
>
> – *Email from the facilitator to Prerna* ❞

selected the work of a classmate who was known to do well in class. She graded carefully, giving full marks (2/2) for one answer, but assigning 4/5 for another. When asked to explain why she had awarded the said marks, Priya first replied simply, 'She has a good handwriting.' Upon being nudged further, Priya observed that *the student's answer was backed by evidence*, and that *there were no spelling mistakes*. Prerna asked Priya how she could tell that there were no spelling mistakes. 'I *know* when a spelling is wrong,' pronounced Priya, firmly. 'Also, she has answered to the point. By looking at her answer, I understood what she wanted to say.' Priya had compared the allotted marks with how much the student had written, which made perfect sense. Prerna thus found that this exercise really worked.

How Self-Aware Is the Erring Student?

As was evident from Priya's identification of her peer's errors, students are often more aware of what is incorrect than teachers may realise. In fact, there were several insights to be gleaned from this exercise.

Firstly, a student (Priya) who frequently made spelling errors was also confident that she knew 'when a spelling was wrong'. This begs the question: why, then, does she err if she already knows when a spelling is incorrect? Of course, reasons could vary depending upon the content, Priya's mood, the situation, etc. But there is a powerful takeaway for any teacher here: that an erring student cannot be dismissed as 'ignorant' of the content. Mistakes are seldom made deliberately; but *that something is a mistake can be easily spotted by many.*

Secondly, phasing out of self-awareness, in order to spot another's errors and only later zero in on one's own errors, proved to be effective in this case. Indeed, this is the fundamental premise of Nobel Laureate Daniel Kahneman's book *Thinking, Fast and Slow*: '... it is easier to recognise other people's mistakes than our own.'

Identifying and Revisiting the Teacher's Own Assumptions

During Prerna's period of research, the authorities at her school once came up with a specific guideline for the teachers that encouraged them to answer worksheets or tests before (or after) administering them. Prerna liked the idea, and applied it for a quiz that she had set for her fifth graders. Figure 10 shows a question (from the quiz) which no one in the class had been able to answer properly (and consequently none had scored well on it). When she tried to answer the question herself, to her amazement, she found that even she could not come up with an adequate answer! She also examined the marks allotted and realised that she had set aside too many marks for this answer, which could only be brief. However, she noted that if she changed the question slightly (to read 'What do you think about Mig's parents?'), then it opened up the possibility of writing a more detailed answer.

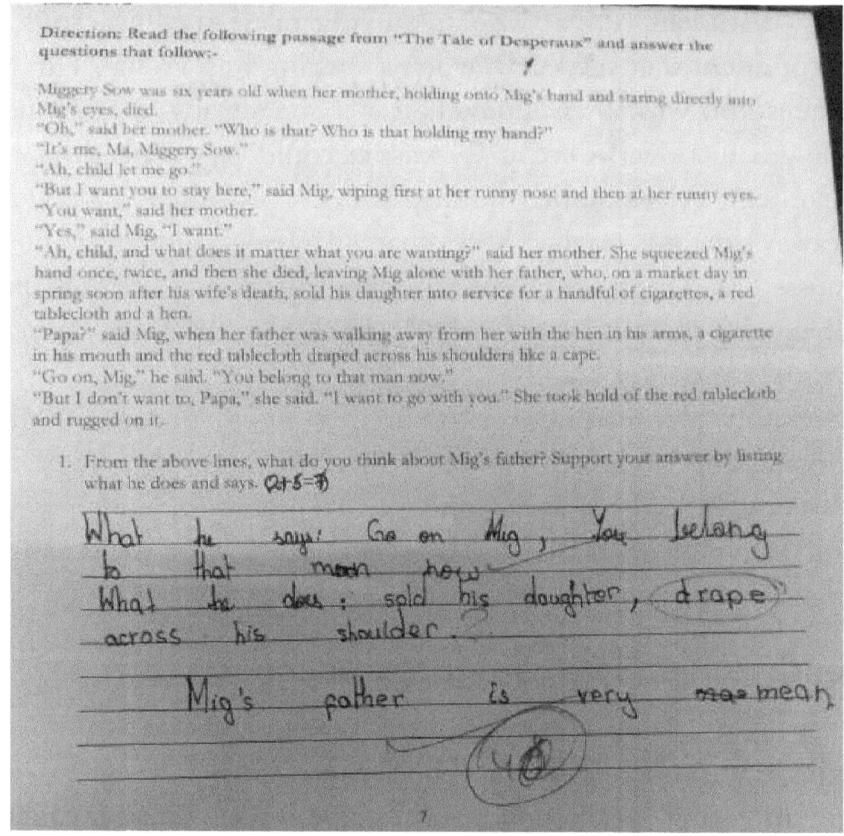

Figure 10: Learning to frame a question

In locating some questions that Prerna herself could not answer, she came face to face with an unreasonable demand that was being placed on the answerer! Realising your own mistake is a very powerful realisation to dawn on a teacher. Thus, a very important learning for Prerna was that *she should frame a question for the students only after first ascertaining that she could answer it herself.*

Another valuable lesson for Prerna through the course of this programme was about her own assumptions regarding students. That is, though she had always known 'Begin from where the learner is' as a teaching principle, she still assumed that students should come to Grade V with the knowledge of all that was taught to them in Grade IV; or that they *should know* 'this, this and this' by Grade V. As she worked through the Reflective Learner Programme, she realised that this is not always necessary or possible – and that gradually they would all learn. Also, if they did not know basic concepts, what was the use of her assuming that they *should know* them? Therefore, instead of focusing on assumptions, she now wanted to *start from where they were*. She could now reconcile that

> The RL Programme helped me reflect on myself and on my teaching. Now I always set my questions and I first answer them, then I give it to my students.
>
> – Prerna's email to the facilitator

there were gaps in this knowledge; and therefore, she took pains to address these gaps.

This study also prompted Prerna to question her prior perception of a student's awareness of what is correct and incorrect. As mentioned earlier, Prerna observed that even students who did not spell correctly were able to point out the spelling errors in another's work. This was an observation with many layers to unravel: When a student does not write correctly, is that indicating that (s)he does not know what is correct? Or that (s)he is aware of what is correct but is – for some reason – unable to write it correctly?

Another assumption that Prerna had held before embarking on this study was that such a project would demand too much of her time. She wondered if stepping down to the level of students with a weaker grasp of even the basic concepts would be far too time-consuming. But through her action research she realised that the answer was 'No'. In fact, this exercise actually helped the teacher as well as these students, as both tried to put in extra effort; and consequently, the transformation was observed at both ends. With such students, she avoided the usual route of giving homework on the lesson taught in class. Instead, she adopted the strategy of one-on-one interactions. To her surprise, she found that this demanded only a three-week investment of one-on-one time with them, after which they seemed more or less on par with the rest.

Students Taking Charge of Their Progress

After three months, Prerna asked each of the three struggling students to set specific goals for their self-improvement. Figure 11 shows a chart of goals, made with the help of the teacher. By enabling the students to set goals for themselves, Prerna attempted to subtly *shift the onus from herself (teacher) to the student.*

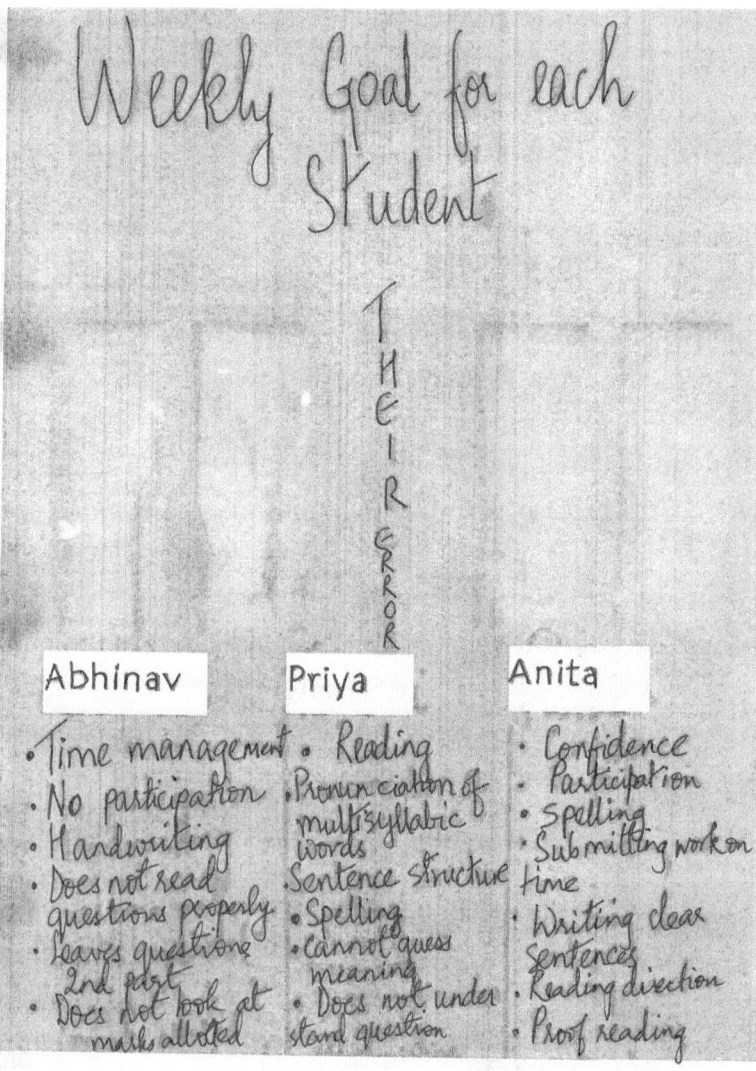

Figure 11: Charter of goals

Once each student had committed to working towards a certain goal, the demand to get there no longer had to keep coming from the teacher. Instead, the students became more self-aware of their own commitment and slowly worked towards it. At the end of the research, Prerna entered the progress of these students against the same individual goals shown in Figure 11. Table 4 illustrates her report.

Table 4: Progress vs goals

Abhinav	Priya	Anita
Time management – Perfect now! No problem.	*Reading* – Does not skip words now; does not fumble; and makes efforts. *Pronunciation of multisyllabic words* – Breaking up the words into bits helped her to slowly pronounce them correctly – in two months	*Reading* – Participates actively in various reading activities.
Participation – Slow kid, but participates nowadays.	*Spelling* – Strategy has worked, progressing, not as good as others yet.	*Spelling* – Can identify all spelling mistakes, doesn't always write correctly.
Handwriting – Erratic	*Understanding questions* – Understands the question now (underlines key words).	*Writing clear sentences* – Up to 70% better now.
Reading instructions carefully; leaving out questions; and understanding the marks allotted – Improved in the first two, but not the last (interestingly, almost all the students have not yet figured how much to write for the marks allotted)	*Reading and guessing the meaning* – Has started inferring meanings, at least she tries nowadays.	*Proofreading for comma, full stop and question mark* – 50% progress.

Contd...

Abhinav	Priya	Anita
Proofreading for comma, full stop and question mark – No longer a struggling student! Does not need my support anymore.	*Sentence structure* – Not that clear, but has started writing simple sentences; so, there is some improvement.	*Reading instructions carefully* – Started reading them. *Submitting work on time* – 100% progress.

Moving out of the Old Errors

At the end of the research, Prerna listed the typical errors made by the three struggling students at the start of this programme, as well as the observations about their progress, as shown in Table 5.

Table 5: Comparison of initial difficulties vs progress made by the end of the programme

Student	Type of error	Progress details during August–December 2016
Abhinav	• Unable to spot his own errors. • Unable to form clear sentences. • Makes careless spelling mistakes. • Copies incorrect spellings from questions. • Makes capitalisation errors (concept taught in the class). • Makes many punctuation errors in written work.	• He is able to spot the mistakes now. • He can understand the sentences from a given text, but writes sentences that are unclear and grammatically incorrect. • He has mastered the spellings of many words. • He has shown progress with capitalisation. • He is getting better at punctuating his writing, too, through reinforced learning. • He speaks fast, but uses tenses correctly and does not mix genders. His spoken skills are good, and he is a good reader, but sometimes he finds it difficult to write correctly.

Student	Type of error	Progress details during August-December 2016
Priya	• Unable to understand any given passage. • Answers whatever she wants. • Unable to understand questions. • Does not proofread her work. • Makes too many spelling mistakes. • Makes many grammatical errors (verb-tense consistency, run on sentences, present-past-future) • Repeats words (e.g. he *told told* me). • Answers are not connected to the topic. • Unable to apply the concept taught in the class. • Writes in a haphazard manner.	• She has improved, and made a jump of 14 reading levels[3]. • She has made significant improvement with listening, as well as speaking with clarity and correctness. • She proofreads better now, but needs more practice in this. • Her spelling is improving, though she still has some way to go. • She has responded well to the strategy of correcting another's work, and has shown an understanding of the correspondence between marks allotted and answers. It has also had an impact on her self-evaluation skills. • She has started inferring meanings. • She understands the questions, is able to underline the key words.
Anita	• Makes capitalisation errors. • Unable to form proper sentences. • Does not understand what she is writing. • Does not understand questions. • Makes spelling errors. • Makes grammatical mistakes. • Answers verbally, but while writing, able to write little or nothing. • Makes punctuation errors. • Takes a long time to complete her work, but writes very little.	• She has improved, but there is still a lot left to do. • She now writes simple and clear sentences. • She does her homework independently. • She has actively started participating in reading activities. • She is able to spot all her spelling mistakes, but still does not write correctly. • Even though all the teachers have seen signs of progress in her, she still needs constant monitoring and push. • She always submits her work on time now.

[3] Taktse International uses the Fountas and Pinnell guided reading programme (http://www.fountasandpinnellleveledbooks.com/aboutleveledtexts.aspx), and students are accordingly tested for their current reading level three times in a year. At the end of the academic year, these test records are sent by the current teacher to the next year's teacher for appropriate follow-up

Overall Consolidation of Changes

A four-month journey thus turned into a reflective one for both the learners and the teacher (Prerna). The following are some of the important milestones in this journey:

1. Prerna examined her own assumptions about students' mindsets, and realised how any impression that she carries about them gets conveyed wordlessly to them – and consequently impacts their behaviour.

2. She noticed that a student who made many mistakes was able to spot them in *another student's* work. This brought home to her with great force that even a student who errs may not necessarily be unaware of what is correct: the mistake could have been made due to reasons other than ignorance.

3. She re-examined her assumptions about what students 'should know' when they come to her class, and acknowledged the meaninglessness of assuming that all children should possess a certain pre-requisite knowledge when they come to her class.

4. With students having a weaker grasp of basic concepts, she avoided the usual route of giving homework on the lesson taught in class. Instead, she adopted the strategy of sitting with them, one-on-one, and beginning *from where they currently were*. To her surprise, she found that this demanded only a three-week investment (thereafter, they were almost on par with the rest). She noted that working with such students was a great *learning opportunity for her* – as a teacher – for she learnt even as she helped them.

5. She began to appreciate the trait of freely making mistakes as well as acknowledging them.

6. She examined her own process of framing questions for the students. Her turning point came when she failed to adequately answer a question that she had set for her class. This led her to resolving to adopt the practice of always

attempting to answer questions that she set for her class, before expecting them to answer the same.

7. She also realised specific difficulties that individual students faced and saw the power of making them cognisant of their own blocks.

8. She invested efforts in getting children to take the onus for their own growth, by having them prepare their individual spelling lists, set their own goals, etc.

9. She acquired several strategies along the way, e.g. reading aloud in changing tones so as to catch the punctuation therein, allowing students to infer the meaning of what they have read – thus, empowering them to read, guess, infer and so on.

10. Students overcame their fear of making mistakes and were released from any guilt or shame over making mistakes.

11. Students began to take note of their mistakes and realised that they were capable of correcting them.

12. Simple (yet powerful shifts) could be seen in students: taking care to read the question properly, reading aloud without fumbling, mastering spellings, using capitals correctly, answering a question according to the allotted marks, understanding the question asked by underlining the key words, etc.

13. A notoriously laid back and slow student (Abhinav) became so good at time management that he moved out of the 'struggling student' category in less than four months.

14. Students began taking the onus for their own learning in a remarkably short period, simply by being led into a systematic examination of their mistakes – and therefore, the workings of their own minds.

15. All students of Grade V showed an interest in mastering spellings, while the three struggling students displayed visible shifts in their levels of motivation and certain skills. Shifts in these three students were confirmed by other teachers of this class as well.

A Continuing Journey ...

All too often, so many students are trapped in the lonely corner of experiencing difficulties but not knowing how to articulate the nature of these difficulties, let alone correcting them. To top this, of course, are the typically shameful burdens of being branded 'poor performer', 'low achiever', 'not up to the mark', etc. Freed from such humiliating consequences, this work shows that even young students' struggles can be overcome in a remarkably short period. Prerna's study is proof of the same. In giving them a valid platform to air their views on what they perceive as 'right' and 'wrong', students find that acknowledging and correcting their mistakes is stripped of shame and guilt.

Whether any of the shifts described – in the teacher and students – are powerful enough to be sustained is something that only time can tell.

MATHEMATICS IN SLOW MOTION

Mathematics is a subject that demands sequential thinking and application of formulae. Unfortunately, it is very easy for a student to memorise the formulae, and mechanically run through all the steps – without having a clear understanding of *the reasons behind each step*. There is always the lure of quickly arriving at the right answer, after all. Naturally, this leads to learners being slotted as 'weak' or 'proficient' based on their scores in maths tests. This aspect makes it very difficult for a maths teacher to nurture a thorough understanding of even the basic mathematical concepts. Nonetheless, it also provides an opportunity to explore or delve deeper into the mind of a learner. Thus, this chapter takes the aforementioned challenge as the initial point of enquiry, and details an account of a teacher-researcher who prioritised *mathematical thinking* over the right answer, *systematic exposition* over speed and *understanding the mind of a student* over judging him/her as 'weak or proficient'.

The Teacher-Researcher

At the time of conducting this research, M Gopalakrishnan was teaching mathematics to Grades VIII, IX and X in The Peepal Grove School, Sadum, Andhra Pradesh. Gopi (as he is known in the school) began his research into the mistakes made by students of Grade VIII  towards the end of the academic year 2016-17. He completed his research by March 2018.

Gopi had been grappling with the challenge of teaching maths according to the Indian Certificate of Secondary Education (ICSE) syllabus to eighth graders whose fundamentals were very shaky: some had not even understood the concept of place value, others were unsure of decimals and fractions and still others could solve problems correctly without really appreciating the underlying rationale. In 2017-18, the seeds of his research were sown when he participated in the Reflective Learner Programme (RLP) for a period of ten months with the intent of finding a solution to this challenge, and in particular, because he wanted 'to get into the mind of a student' (his own words). Fighting the prevalent emphasis on speed and the right answer, he has been successfully attempting to systematically erode this bias with his innovative strategies and relentless pursuit of probing the thinking behind every student's answer.

Preparing the Ground

Testing waters, he first decided to focus on seven students of Grade VIII who were visibly struggling with mathematics. He called these seven students aside to take their consent and briefly explained to them his research concept. He informed them of the benefits of participating in such an exercise, and that it would also require them to take out time beyond class hours. All the seven students agreed to participate in the study.

In January 2017, Gopi conducted an initial test to identify errors made by these seven participants while carrying out simple numerical calculations. For this purpose, he designed a worksheet with about 20 questions, where there was plenty of scope to make arithmetical errors, and where he concentrated only on the basic arithmetic operations – addition, subtraction, multiplication and division – on numbers. (For a sample worksheet, see Appendix.)

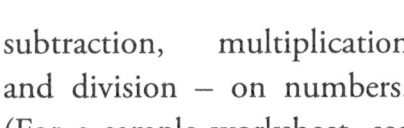

I can see that the children are motivated by this. I am able to get an idea of their (mis)understanding. This further helps me to decide my teaching and testing methodology. I am really happy to see the results of this exercise. I am also happy that you've given me total freedom to do it in the way I think.

- Email from Gopi to the facilitator

I am so happy that you have found your initial foray into 'Missed Takes' research to be worth your while. I look forward to some interesting results from a dedicated maths teacher like you. As for your finding your own way of moving forward, that is precisely the whole idea. If you read the sample chapter that I sent you, that teacher did the same.

All teachers who participate in this programme find their own way of examining their students' mistakes, so you can rest assured that that is how you too will proceed.

Each one has their style and each class has its unique flavour. That is why ONE formula or methodology cannot ever be the way forward.

- Email from the facilitator to Gopi

While administering this worksheet to each of the seven participants, Gopi told them that they were not allowed to ask each other, or even him, for help. Although no time limit had been given to them, he found that they usually took about 30 to 40 minutes to complete each worksheet. He corrected the completed worksheets by simply inserting a tick or a cross against each solution. However, he made a private note of each student's performance in his own register. In the next class, he returned the worksheets, and asked each one if they could spot any of their errors; simultaneously, he worked out every single problem on the blackboard. He also asked them to examine what had prompted them to make a particular error and to articulate their thought process, facilitating the articulation process wherever needed.

Gopi admits that it took time for some of the student-participants to understand what was expected of them. He nudged their self-examination process by asking the following questions:

✦ What is the mistake in this solution?
✦ In what sense is it 'wrong'?
✦ Can you check and tell me?

As they thought and answered, he systematically noted down all their responses. (A few sample responses are listed after Table 1 in the next section.)

He persisted with this same exercise for another four worksheets (a total of 20 questions in each worksheet, 5 for each mathematical operation), with the same seven students. The same level of difficulty was also maintained for all the five worksheets, which were administered once a week. (All he did was change the numbers in the 20 problems of every worksheet.) He minimised variation between worksheets so as to reinforce learning and enhance conquering of errors.

Once the worksheets were submitted, he would correct them; and then call the students the next day during 'telephone calling time'[1] for a discussion. For each student, it took Gopi 20 minutes to run through the corrected sheet, as well as to discuss the possible reasons for their errors therein. Thus, Gopi had to put in an extra two and a half hours per week, apart from his usual class hours. This entire process took about four weeks.

---

[1] The Peepal Grove School is a residential school, and students are allotted a certain time of day for making/receiving long distance telephone calls to/from their families.

Preliminary Findings

Gopi compared the number of errors made by each of the seven students, in four of the five worksheets, and tabulated them as follows (see Table 1):

Table 1: Number of errors made in each worksheet

Student no.	Number of errors			
	Worksheet 1	Worksheet 2	Worksheet 3	Worksheet 4
1	8	6	1	1
2	6	4	6	5
3	10	7	6	1
4	9	9	6	5
5	9	10	8	11
6	3	4	2	0
7	9	3	4	3

As can be seen from the Table 1, barring Student 5 (a new student, having joined only in 2017, with a huge lacuna in basic mathematical concepts), all others began moving in the direction of making fewer errors by the end of the fourth worksheet. Gopi probed deeper by having the seven students examine the reasons for their different errors. By the end of this five-week cycle of worksheets reinforcing simple arithmetic, many realisations surfaced for both the students and the teacher.

> My time with every child is very limited. This process of designing and transacting such experiments allows me to see their thinking - without taking much more of my time.
>
> *- Gopi in a conversation with the facilitator*

Some of the observations made by the students about their own work are as follows:

✦ For the same sign, I should have added. But I subtracted.

✦ I put the decimal point in the wrong place – not concentrating.

✦ I added instead of multiplying.

✦ I didn't see the word 'from'. I know how to do this.

When such an admission came, Gopi would immediately give them another problem in order to assess if they had truly 'got it' – usually, they did. However, Gopi admitted that there was no guarantee that this understanding would last until the next worksheet!

The teacher's discovery lay in the extent of reinforcement of fundamentals that was found to be necessary – indeed, Gopi remarked that although he had known that the fundamentals of these students were shaky, he had had no idea that they were *so weak*! For instance, there were several instances that highlighted a lack of understanding about subtraction (particularly borrowing) and place value in these thirteen- or fourteen-year-old participants. Table 2 illustrates his findings.

Table 2: Description of errors

Error no.	Description of error
1	Subtracting mechanically without having understood the concept of borrowing
2	Unaware that each placeholder can only hold a single digit
3	Not knowing that subtraction has to be done each time from the digit above the one below
4	While multiplying, inserting the tens digit in the answer in place of the unit's digit
5	Overlooking the sign before each number
6	While dividing, forgetting to put zero in the answer if the number brought down is smaller than the divisor
7	Copying digits illegibly and thus adding to existing errors in the next step

Further, he realised that the main issue was a student's ability to pay attention. In other words, learning and retention happen only when students pay attention. To cite just one example, Gopi noted that when one student took 10 minutes to review his paper, he scored 20 out of 20.

Moreover, Gopi restrained his urge to simply show the students their mistakes, or scold them. Instead, he asked them, 'What was your thought process while problem-solving?' Or told them, 'Illustrate to me how you got the answer.' The entire exercise thus helped Gopi peek into a student's mind, which was his original intent.

Once this initial exploration was over, examinations and end-of-year work prevented Gopi from further continuing his research with the same batch of students. However, this effort proved very valuable when he launched into a full-fledged study shortly after (described in the next section).

Designing and Implementing Strategies in the New Academic Year

The aforementioned exercise based on simple arithmetic worksheets provided Gopi with enough food for thought. So, in the new academic year 2017-18, with a fresh batch of students in Grade VIII, he began to devise ways of probing all his students' minds, right from the start. He called these exercises his 'experiments'. Nine of these experiments are described as follows (of which the last five are diagnostic tests):

1. **Spot the error:** Gopi prepared a worksheet that contained 23 arithmetical problems guised as solutions. In other words, he had deliberately inserted an error into each and every one of the problems. Some examples of these erroneous problems are as follows:

   a) $-20 - 13 = 7$ b) $\frac{23}{4} = 3\frac{4}{5}$ c) $5\frac{1}{4} = \frac{20}{4}$

   He crafted these errors mostly by drawing from the mistakes made by the students, with a few new errors thrown in from his own imagination. The worksheet was administered as a one-hour test where students had to spot the errors. (Figure 1 shows a sample worksheet.)

Worksheet – Grade VIII

Locate the errors and correct them.

Q1 $624 \div 3 = 28$

Q2 $84 - 59 = 35$

Q3 $\dfrac{45}{35} = \dfrac{5}{7}$

Q4 $\dfrac{30 \times 20}{60} = \dfrac{3 \times 2}{6}$

Q5 $\dfrac{10\cancel{8}}{2\cancel{0}}$

Q6 $\dfrac{1}{4} + \dfrac{1}{3} = \dfrac{1+1}{4+3} = \dfrac{2}{7}$

Q7 $-20 - 13 = 7$

Q8 $-5 - 3 = +8$

Q9 $\dfrac{1}{4} + \dfrac{1}{3} = \dfrac{1}{12} + \dfrac{1}{12} = \dfrac{2}{12}$

Q10 $5\dfrac{1}{4} = \dfrac{20}{4}$

Q11 $\dfrac{23}{4} = 3\dfrac{4}{5}$

Q12 $\dfrac{5}{25} = \dfrac{1}{5} = 5$

Q13 $\dfrac{14}{25} \div \dfrac{7}{10} = \dfrac{25}{14} \times \dfrac{7}{10}$

Q14 $\dfrac{14}{25} \div \dfrac{10}{7} = \dfrac{2}{5} \div \dfrac{2}{1} = \dfrac{4}{5}$

Q15 $\dfrac{12}{15} = \dfrac{x}{5}$;

$12x = 15 \times 5$

Q16 Express 12 as a per cent of 3:

$\dfrac{3}{12} \times 100 = 25\%$

Q17 Subtract 12 from 9:

$12 - 9 = 3$

Figure 1: Sample worksheet for locating and correcting errors

Moreover, here's an interesting twist: he not only asked them to spot the error but also *invited a description of each error,* which, he admitted, the lazier ones did not bother to do. The descriptions brought to the fore the precise step(s) that were missing (or incorrect) in the students' logic. For example, while describing a long-division problem, many omitted mentioning that a zero is inserted in the quotient when the digit of the dividend is smaller than the divisor. And only later is the next digit brought down (e.g. in 624 ÷ 6, the quotient is 104 as 2 < 6). Instead, they simply stated that the two digits of the dividend would have to be brought down (hence, in the above example, 624 ÷ 6, their logic would indicate that the quotient be 14, instead of 104).

In another instance, the students' use of 'carry over' instead of 'borrow' for subtraction highlighted their lack of awareness of precise terminology.

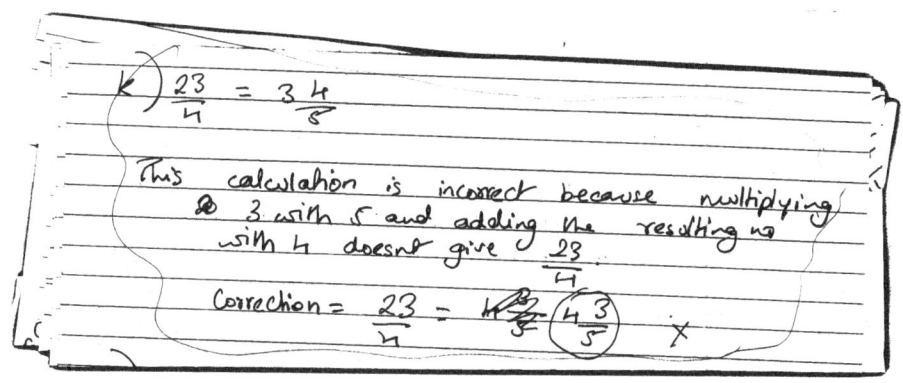

Figure 2: Error analysis by a student

In Figure 2, despite his written statement revealing the right logic, the student has interchanged the digits in the last step – thus showing his lack of focus on the denominator. This student understood that verification was successful in identifying a mistake, but in so doing, he overlooked the denominator.

Thus, this exercise was helping the students to become more aware of their mistakes. And the intent was strengthened further by the overall results, which were very heartening for Gopi: out of 22 students, only 4 had difficulty in identifying the errors. All the rest had spotted 20 or more out of 23 errors. Mistakes are, therefore, slowly weeded out through this strategy.

2. **Delineate four stages**: For this crucial experiment, Gopi prepared a worksheet and asked the students to solve the given problems by delineating for each the following 'four stages':

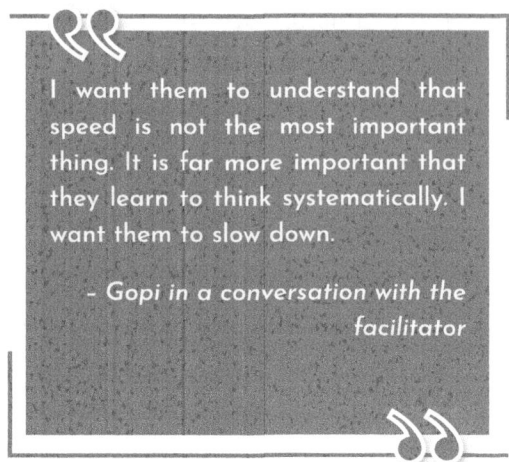

> I want them to understand that speed is not the most important thing. It is far more important that they learn to think systematically. I want them to slow down.
>
> *– Gopi in a conversation with the facilitator*

   ✦ Information given in the problem
   ✦ What has to be found
   ✦ A simple plan for solving the problem
   ✦ Solution (implementing the plan)

Gopi began by showing the class a few examples of this format. Anticipating their reactions to the rigorous plan, he also explained to them that they needed to invest this kind of time and effort in order to gain speed and competence in the long run. Gopi noted with gratification that they were convinced enough to try. It was however a strict regimen; and many groaned under it, or found it boring. Nonetheless, his confidence was well-founded, as the results indicated that about 75 per cent of the class had 'got it'. (In fact, it was so successful that he began the trial exercise in Grade X as well.) The same students continued to struggle, however.

3. **Write the next step**: Gopi administered a worksheet with 40 questions (based on content that had been taught thus far). In this experiment, the students were asked to simply write the step *subsequent* to the one given in the worksheet; the *entire* problem was not to be solved. (Figure 3 shows a sample worksheet.) If some students could not stop themselves from going ahead and working out more than just the next step, Gopi marked that answer as incorrect, even if the steps were correctly executed. This was part of his effort to slow down the thought process of the students.

Grade VIII – Worksheet

Write the next step.

Q1 $+30 - 25 + 15 - 6$

Q2 $25 \div 5 \times 3$

Q3 $12 \div \frac{1}{4}$ *of* 24

Q4 $5(-3 - 5)$

Q5 $3\frac{1}{2} + 7\frac{1}{3}$

Q6 $\frac{3}{4} + \frac{1}{6}$

Q7 $\frac{3}{12} + \frac{5}{12}$

Q8 $\frac{11}{15} - \frac{8}{15}$

Q9 $\frac{25}{35}$

Q10 $\frac{25}{4}$

Q11 $\frac{12}{14} \times \frac{7}{18}$

Q12 $\frac{3}{5} \times \frac{7}{4}$

Q13 $\frac{25}{28} \div \frac{10}{14}$

Q14 $\sqrt{225}$

Q15 8^2

Q16 7^3

Q17 $\sqrt[3]{216}$

Q18 Show a direct variation

Q19 Show an inverse variation

Q20 $\frac{4}{5} = \frac{x}{15}$

Figure 3: Sample worksheet for writing the next step

4. **Reflect on the problem-solving process**: In order to address the fact that students swiftly turned in correct answers without revealing their thought process in arriving at the answer, Gopi asked them to not only solve a problem but also follow it up by explaining *why and how* they went about solving it that way. By so doing, Gopi showed that he was more interested in knowing what went on in a student's mind than in simply marking an answer correct.

Thus, in this experiment, he did not demand from them a plan beforehand, instead he asked for a reflection post the completion of the worksheet. Figure 4 illustrates one such reflection.

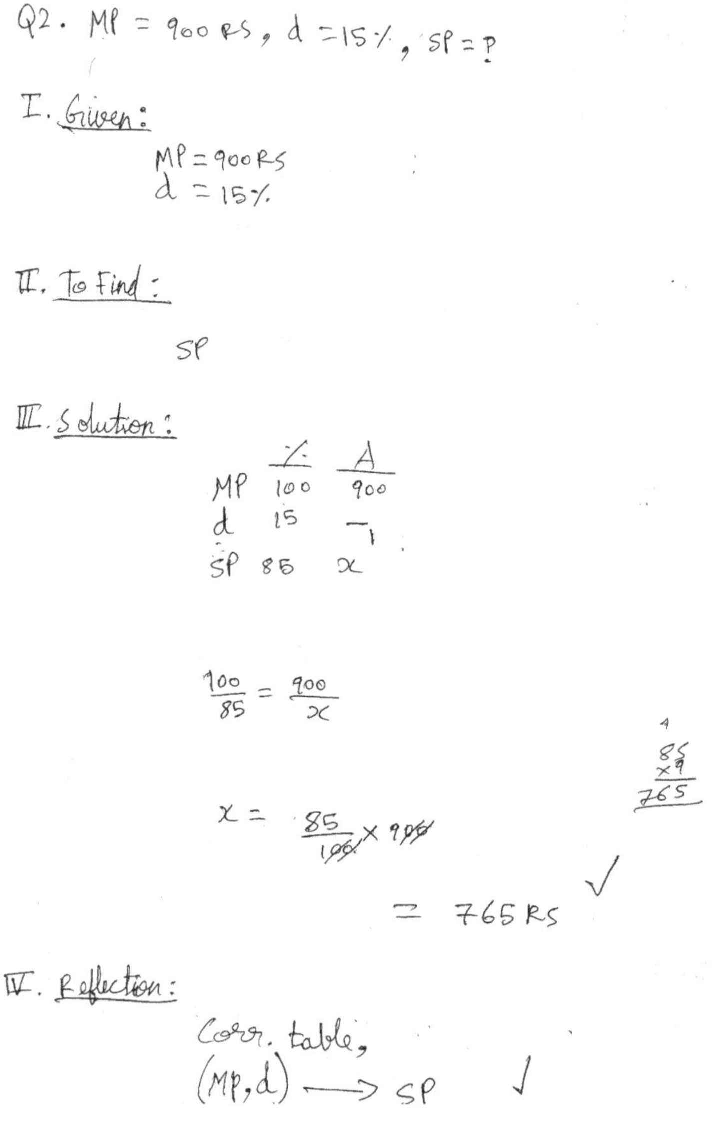

Q2. MP = 900 RS, d = 15%, SP = ?

I. Given:

MP = 900 RS
d = 15%

II. To find:

SP

III. Solution:

$$\begin{array}{c|cc} & \% & A \\ MP & 100 & 900 \\ d & 15 & \\ SP & 85 & x \end{array}$$

$$\frac{100}{85} = \frac{900}{x}$$

$$\begin{array}{r} 85 \\ \times 9 \\ \hline 765 \end{array}$$

$$x = \frac{85}{100} \times 900$$

$$= 765 \, RS \quad \checkmark$$

IV. Reflection:

Corr. table,

$$(MP, d) \longrightarrow SP \quad \checkmark$$

* MP – Marked Price; SP – Selling Price; d – Discount

Figure 4: Scanned image of a student's reflection

This exercise was similar to the Four Stages experiment, but it differed in that the student reflected *after* completing the worksheet, and clearly articulated the thought process employed while solving each problem. This enabled the teacher to sift out those solutions where the right answer had been arrived at through an incorrect process. Thus, the demand for rigour was being increased gradually, and it began to penetrate the thinking of each student before as well as after completing the exercises.

5. **Display understanding, but show no calculations**[2]: In an effort to find out *how students think about a problem*, Gopi prepared a worksheet containing a table with 53 rows (each row listing a separate problem) and two columns – the first titled 'data', and the second 'what can be found from such data'. The students had to look at the data provided in the first column and ask themselves: *From this given data, what can be found?* For example, if the entry in the first column was Cost Price = ₹ 100 and Selling Price = ₹ 120, then Profit = ₹ 20 needed to be entered in the second column. (A couple of such examples were first demonstrated in class.)

   The worksheet thus contained a total of 53 questions, and was administered in 30 to 45 minutes. The overall performance of the Grade VIII students in this experiment turned out to be rather good: for instance, 20 out of 22 students scored more than 60 per cent.

6. **Apply the appropriate formulae**[3]: For this experiment, Gopi prepared a worksheet wherein students were asked to merely *write out the formula* for solving a given problem (e.g. 'Given Cost Price and Selling Price, which formula is needed to find Profit?'). This worksheet was also administered in 35-40 minutes.

7. **Specify the data that is needed**: In another experiment, Gopi prepared worksheets where the students had to provide missing

---

[2] Experiment 5 was completed by the eighth graders within one prep (75 minutes).
[3] Experiment 6 was completed by the eighth graders within one prep (75 minutes).

data for each of the given questions (e.g. 'What is the data that is required to find Profit?'). Gopi's intent in conducting such a test was to prod the students to look at a problem from more than just the angle of 'How do I solve this correctly?' Instead, he invested efforts in getting students to examine a problem with a more clinical eye: for example, by asking themselves what sort of data they would need *before* beginning to solve it. Gopi's intent here was also to empower the students to draw a generic insight from examining a particular problem.

8. **Plan only:** The penultimate experiment required the students to draw up only their plan for solving a given problem. Figure 5 illustrates one such sample. In alignment with the earlier experiments, this was also intended to get the students to consolidate their thought process before speeding towards the right answer.

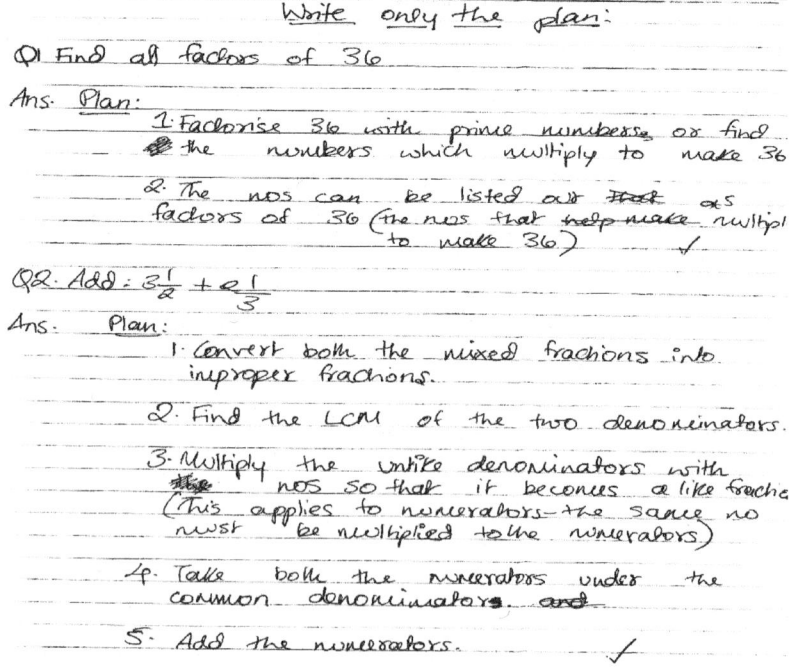

Figure 5: What's your plan?

9. **Write reasons for geometrical statements:** In the final experiment, Gopi designed a worksheet with geometrical statements and asked the students to justify them by giving reasons. The intent here was to get the students to think before they wrote anything, as he had found that most often, they would simply write without thinking. Figure 6 shows a sample of a completed worksheet, wherein the student has specified the reason for each of the given seven statements.

Processes that Were Set in Motion

By breaking down the steps in solving any problem, there were several consequences that Gopi intended. Some of these are summarised as follows:

1. It is always easier to spot errors in another's work, than to see them in one's own. Learning to spot errors in another's work was intended to slowly lead students to recognise errors in their own work. Gopi discerned a noticeable change in students' attitude towards their own mistakes after they had spotted errors in his *Spot the Error* worksheet (experiment 1). This exercise took away the fear of mistakes from them and they understood that it was 'ok' to make mistakes, and that one can always learn from them. In any case, the students were very happy to look for mistakes committed by the teacher – sometimes deliberate and at others, inadvertent!

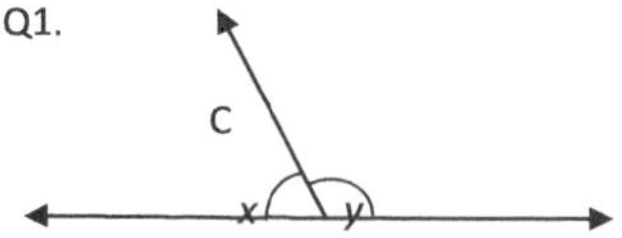

x and *y* form a linear pair.

Q1.

Ans: <u>Yes, adjacent angles on a straight line form a linear pair.</u>

Q2.

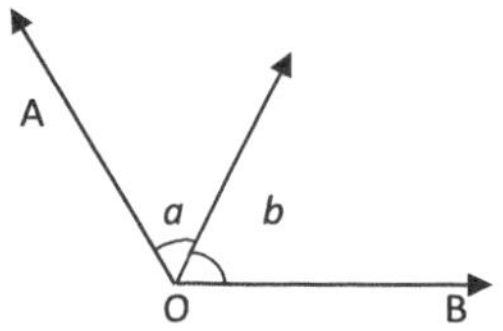

a and *b* do not form a linear pair.

Ans: <u>It is not a linear pair, because AOB is not a straight line.</u>

Q3.

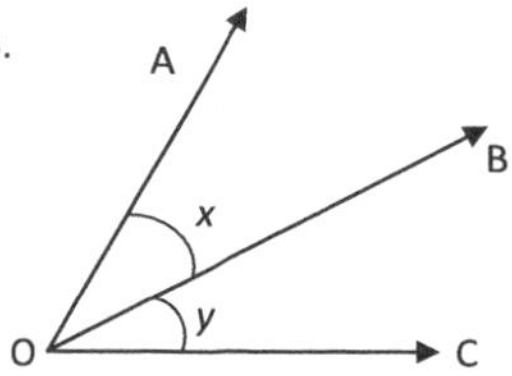

x and *y* are adjacent angles.

Ans: <u>They are adjacent angles because they have a common arm and vertex, and they add up to ∠AOC.</u>

Q4.

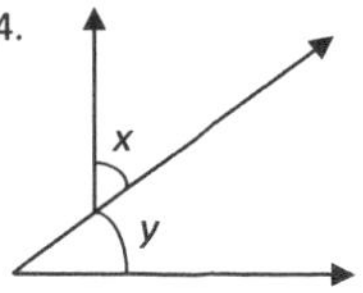

x and *y* are not adjacent angles.
Ans: <u>They are not adjacent angles because they don't have a common vertex.</u>

Q5.

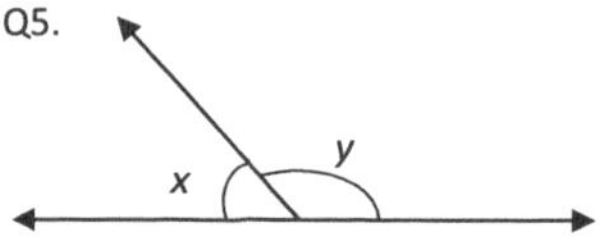

$x + y = 180^0$

Ans: <u>*x* and *y* are a linear pair, and linear pair of angles add up to 180°.</u>

Q6.

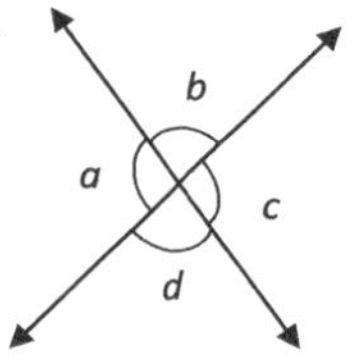

$a + b = 180°$, $a = c$, $b = d$, and $c + d = 180°$

Ans: <u>$a + b = 180^0$, because *a* and *b* are a linear pair; and linear pair of angles add up to 180°.</u>
<u>$a = c$, because they are vertically opposite angles.</u>
<u>$b = d$, because they are vertically opposite angles.</u>
<u>$c + d = 180^0$, because *c* and *d* are a linear pair; and linear pair of angles add up to 180°.</u>

Q7.

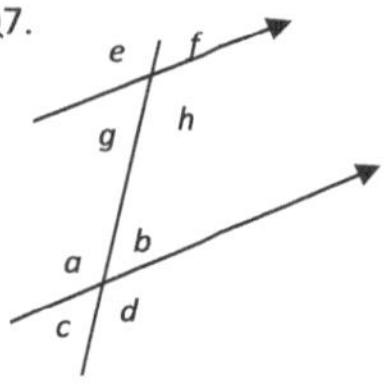

$b + h = 180^0$, $e = h$; $e + f = 180^0$; $g = b$; and $a = h$

Ans: <u>$b + h = 180^0$, because co-interior angles add up to 180°.</u>
<u>$e = h$, vertically opposite angles are equal.</u>
<u>$e + f = 180^0$, linear pair of angles add up to 180°.</u>
<u>$g = b$, alternate interior angles are equal.</u>

Figure 6: Sample worksheet for geometrical reasoning

2. Having recognised an error, the next step was to articulate the reasons for deeming it so. By drawing out explanations from the students (and then discussing the same), Gopi encouraged articulation of reasoning, which is usually bypassed in the rush to arrive at the right answer. As students slowly began to express their reasoning more freely, their fear of 'looking silly' or 'being wrong' slowly decreased. The articulation from the students helped the teacher to understand the level of confusion (or clarity) in their thinking, and take necessary steps to remove the confusion. Based on his impression of their erroneous thinking, he would decide on a strategy for the next class to improve his lectures so as to bring more clarity into their thinking. (Subsequently, Gopi has continued to make it a point in each lecture to articulate the reasons behind each step precisely and clearly. Thus, it has impacted his pedagogy significantly.)

3. Insisting on a description of the four stages was the next step in enhancing the degree of rigour and decreasing the haste in arriving at the right answer. Tiresome as many deemed this exercise to be, it played a huge role in slowing down the students' thinking as well as working through each problem

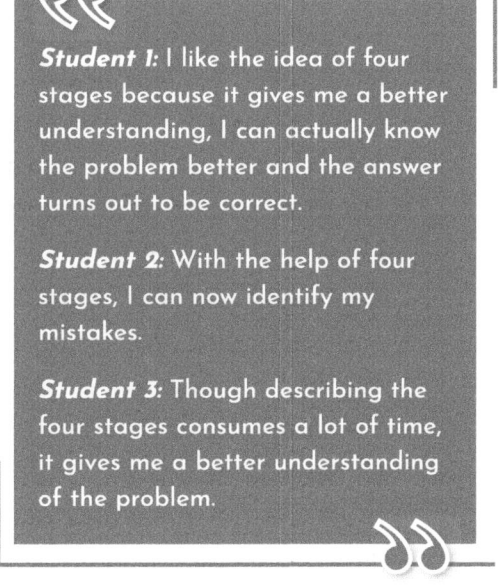

Student 1: I like the idea of four stages because it gives me a better understanding, I can actually know the problem better and the answer turns out to be correct.

Student 2: With the help of four stages, I can now identify my mistakes.

Student 3: Though describing the four stages consumes a lot of time, it gives me a better understanding of the problem.

Figure 7: Student responses

on paper. The three responses by students listed in Figure 7 acknowledge the importance of this method.

4. Nudging students to think about the possible usages of a given set of data gave them a new lens with which to examine a problem. With increasing practice in such an exercise, Gopi intended for them to begin examining a problem by looking at the data and thinking about various outcomes that could emerge from such information. This is one way of encouraging analytical thinking in students.

5. Exercises that pinned students down to simply reading the given first step and then writing *only the next step*; spelling out the formula to be applied; etc. were all ways of *slowing them down*. Gopi broke the problem down into components, so that the student focused on *just one component at a time*. *Thinking* then became more and more apparent – both to the teacher and the student. Its importance was also becoming real to the learner: for the teacher was valuing it enough to administer worksheets which *only* sought to draw out their thinking. A student even commented that each maths class was helping him learn *how to think*; another discovered that he had 'an excellent brain'!

6. Reflection on the manner in which a student had attempted to solve the problem was another way in which the teacher drew out the thinking of the student, while also showing that it was important for him (the teacher) to understand this. In Gopi's experience, children were, in general, focused on just solving a problem and moving on to the next. They seldom stopped to look back and reflect on how they had solved the problem. Therefore, he encouraged them to reflect so that they could see how a particular problem was different from another; recognise the algorithm that each one followed; identify the data from which they could find other information; etc. This, he knew, would help them in drawing out a more general insight from a specific problem and appreciating the richness of each problem. Also, it would strengthen and reinforce their

conceptual as well as procedural understanding. As students did this exercise, they paused to look at the way their minds had worked *during the answering of the problem*, and in so doing, recognised and valued their own thought processes. It, in turn, helped the teacher to assess the level of understanding of each student.

Awakening the Reflective Learner

The Reflective Learner Programme's main intent is the transfer of the onus of learning to students. Through the above experiments, this intent began to be realised as students started to see that there were many different ways in which one could approach maths. This was a significant shift from regarding maths as a subject to be suffered or dreaded. As the year progressed, the teacher could see that the class, as a whole, showed more interest and enthusiasm in doing maths. Even those students who had begun the year experiencing difficulty in solving problems were now eager to take up challenges. They could be seen attempting to solve problems, since the pressure of succeeding had now been taken away from them. They were now freely experimenting with various options, unimpeded by the fear of failing. Overall class participation increased noticeably: more and more students started asking questions to get their doubts cleared, and were eager to answer the questions posed by the teacher. They started to realise the importance of understanding each concept even as they became cognisant of their own mistakes. This was a shift from emphasising the right answer and *only the right answer*. There was a tangible increase in their level of motivation, as is evident from their end-of-year feedback. At the start and end of the year, students were simply asked by their teacher to rate their own shift (if any) in:

+ confidence,
+ interest,

✦ understanding and

✦ skills in maths.

Despite the gradually increasing level of difficulty in content that is natural in any curriculum as the year progresses, all but two of the students rated themselves as having increased understanding, interest, confidence and skills by the end of the year.

Investment of Time by the Teacher

Gopi was given only two grades to teach in the academic year 2017-18, as the Principal of The Peepal Grove School extended her support to him for his research. Therefore, he was able to carry out his study without undue pressure. Although the entire process demanded from him a substantial investment of time at the start, this steadily decreased. For instance, the initial time invested in his error analysis efforts was about 4 hours a week, which reduced to 3 by the fourth week. Preparing worksheets, administering them and checking them so as to provide meaningful feedback to the class took an average of four hours a week. In the case of experiments 4 and 8 above, the investment of time was more from the student's perspective.

Role of Facilitator

The teacher-researcher (Gopi) was fired with his own ideas all through this work; therefore, the role of the facilitator was limited to reading his reports (over email) and making suggestions to gather data. It was largely at the end of the project – when the work had to be collated and written up in its present form – that the facilitator played a more significant role. Documentation was done largely by the facilitator with inputs of actual information and data from the teacher-researcher.

Post-Research Changes in the Teacher's Approach

As a result of this research, Gopi brought into his teaching practice the following long-term changes:

1. He continues to conduct all the experiments and is exploring ways and means of doing so with Grades IX and X.

2. Since the Four Stages experiment was deemed by the students to be time-consuming, he switches between that and a detailing out of their plan – as described in experiment 8, titled 'Plan Only'.

> I am constantly thinking about new ideas to explore: how to improve their understanding, how to make them think, how to make them interested in maths ... It has been a very exciting and fulfilling experience for me.
>
> *- Email from Gopi to the facilitator at the end of the research project*

3. He has discontinued the practice of student-wise error analysis (using worksheets like that shown in the Appendix) as he is realising the same intent through all the aforementioned experiments.

4. He has developed a set of rules that students can memorise after understanding them, like '+ added to + yields +' and '– added to – yields –'; 'never add denominators'; and 'never subtract denominators'.

Post-Research Learnings of the Teacher

The Reflective Learner programme drew out the reflective learner from the teacher as well. As he reflected on the entire research project, Gopi summarised his own takeaways against each of the students' challenges, which are illustrated in Table 3.

Table 3: Teacher's takeaway from students' patterns

S. no.	Observation	Change required in my teaching methodology
1	Even though a student identifies a mistake correctly, he is unable to describe it clearly and precisely.	I can give the students a clear set of rules with a precise description of what is allowed/not allowed in each operation.
2	Students find writing the 'four stages' time consuming.	I will use 'four stages' once in a while; I can ask them to write only the plan instead of all 'four stages'.
3	Students make some repeated and typical mistakes.	• I can make a list of typical mistakes made by students in each topic, and draw their attention to these mistakes while dealing with each topic. • I can create some memory aids to make them remember the correct procedure and avoid errors. • I can frame different questions and examples, where there is a greater likelihood of committing errors and then, bring their attention to the mistakes. • While explaining concepts, I usually stop at giving examples. But now I can give examples and counter examples, e.g. what is a polynomial and what is *not* a polynomial.
4	Students are unable to write the plan clearly and properly.	While solving examples, I can teach them to write plans. For each procedure, I can spell out the steps involved in general terms while teaching. I can then break the 'plan' into subcomponents and teach them and test them. (This is what prompted experiments 5, 6 and 7.)
5	Students don't write all steps.	• I can ask them to tell me the immediate next step even as I am explaining. This way, I can proceed till the end of the problem. • While correcting their work, I can indicate which step is missing.
6	The step written by a student is incomplete.	I can explain to the student what constitutes a 'complete step'. Thereafter, while correcting their work, I can indicate what is missing in a step.

S. no.	Observation	Change required in my teaching methodology
7	Student is able to write the step but doesn't know the reason behind it.	During the lecture, I can explain the reason behind each step and also ask a lot of 'why' questions – so as to make them think about the reason behind each step.
8	Students tend to respond without much thinking.	• I can frequently give them a statement and ask them to state the reason for that. (This is what prompted experiment 9.) • Before beginning any worksheet or exercise, I can ask them to first think about the problems for 20 minutes, formulate the plan in their minds for about 5 to 10 problems and *then* start to solve them. • I can give them just minimum information required while introducing a concept, then throw them a challenge and ask them to figure out how to solve a problem. The high achievers will surely be motivated by this and be willing to stretch themselves. The medium-level achievers will also attempt at their level. The low-level achievers will also start to experience the pull of this process eventually and put in more effort.
9	These experiments have given me just a glimpse of what goes on in a student's mind.	I can design more such worksheets, which will make students articulate their thinking in words, thus making it more transparent.
10	The students have not yet completely understood how I solve a problem.	While lecturing, I can regularly make my thinking transparent to them.

The noteworthy reflection is that in trying to get into each student's mind, the teacher saw the need for students to be able to see the working of the teacher's mind as well!

By the end of this project, Gopi began to incorporate all of the above strategies and is currently engaged in implementing them routinely as part of his teaching practice. The reflective learner, then, is not only the student: so is the teacher!

Post-Research Changes in Student Attitudes

This account exemplifies the transformation that can be wrought in the minds of students even towards an oft-feared subject like mathematics.

All the student-participants of this study were asked to describe their experience of mathematics through the year. At the end of the preliminary four-week study with seven students, the facilitator of the Research Learner Programme met with them. She asked them to describe their experience of mathematics through the year and audio recorded their feedback. All of them expressed their enhanced confidence in maths and their surprise at how far behind they had been at the start. Some were shocked to recall that even basic concepts like place value had eluded them earlier. Needless to say, all of them appreciated the dedicated efforts of their teacher to address the gaps in their understanding.

A few sample responses are as follows:

- ✦ I know my parents have high hopes from me; so earlier I used to feel guilty and embarrassed at my performance. But now I make fewer mistakes, and slowly I am gaining in confidence.
- ✦ Whenever we made mistakes in a problem, *Bhaiyya* asked us to form a similar question and solve it.
- ✦ I was shocked when I couldn't even recall my basics … I had gotten my basics all wrong when I was in first or second grade. Till I did this worksheet, I didn't know that I had not grasped place value. *Bhaiyya*[4] taught me subtraction all over again.
- ✦ At first, I made so many mistakes. I didn't know how to subtract, didn't know place value … He made me do it again … in the third week, he taught me again … by the fourth worksheet, I made fewer mistakes.
- ✦ Now I don't feel bad making mistakes. I have learnt so much from my mistakes.
- ✦ When I checked my answers before turning a worksheet in, it made a big difference.
- ✦ We will take more care in future, because many of our mistakes need not have been made at all.

---

[4] Male teachers are addressed as *Bhaiyya* (elder brother) by students of this school.

I was not interested in maths at the start of this academic year though I was good enough to cope with the syllabus. I am now looking forward to more maths classes as there are many challenges.

I have discovered that I can make formulae on the spot, and so I don't have to memorise them. (But I should stop doing this as it is time consuming.)

I have discovered that in my dream of becoming a software designer/producer, I will have to embrace maths.

I have discovered that Maths is not about calculating numbers but thinking in different ways to find a solution and imagining differently.

The thing that I love about Maths is that its concepts are all related to each other, making it easier.

When I started maths this year, I hated it. I really like maths now because *Bhaiyya* has made it simple and understandable for me.

This year, I experienced maths in a way that I'd never experienced before. It was much more challenging and interesting.

I am not afraid of asking questions anymore, because my enhanced understanding has made all my questions worth asking.

Maths for me, in the start of this academic year, was extremely easy, and hence, boring. Comparatively, it has now become tough, and hence, more interesting and brain teasing. In the start of the year, my confidence level was high. Right now, it is not high, but just enough.

My confidence level was low at the start of the academic year, and I thought I had better start preparing for the exams at the start itself. Now I am quite confident to face the exams.

Maths is definitely going to be a part of my career, and I regained the confidence to become an architect.

I discovered that I am not weak: even I can cope up with the other (good) students.

I have seen how maths can help you in your everyday life and I've changed most of my opinions about maths.

I was extremely scared of maths. My hands would shiver and sweat when I looked at sums. Now I look at it as a challenge! Everything is like a challenge and a mystery. I find it interesting. I like doing maths and it helps me in solving other problems. I am not afraid of getting things wrong. I discovered that I have a very good brain to use!

I have discovered that I am good at maths, and all I need is a little concentration.

I have developed the habit of reading and understanding the question first. I discovered that I can think hard and solve anything with a bit of help.

I have discovered that if you put your interest into a subject, miracles result. I can now see myself doing maths in a way that I never used to before, and I am very happy about it.

I would like to know more about Linear equations and calculus, so that I can come up with an explanation of the construction of a sphere.

Figure 8: Students' feedback at the end of the academic year

✦ Now I have started paying more attention to a question. I understand it better.

✦ Previously, I would carry out the working in my head. Now I show it on paper, and because of this, I don't make as many mistakes.

✦ My only mistakes were carelessness and not concentrating.

✦ This research helped me a lot; and mostly because of the way *Bhaiyya* did it. If there is continuous explanation, we understand better; he explained again and again till we understood.

If such encouraging feedback could come from the pilot group, with whom Gopi engaged for a mere five weeks, it naturally makes one wonder about the feedback of the eighth graders in the academic year 2017-18 (participants of Gopi's full-fledged research). A few sample responses of these students are given in Figure 8.

It is clear from Figure 8 that students acquired new habits, made discoveries about their own abilities and aptitude for maths and expressed delight in being stimulated to think and be challenged. The significance of the realisation that maths is relevant, useful and actually more to do with a way of thinking than mere computation cannot be overstated.

Contrary to popular notions, far from being intimidated by challenge, it is evident that students welcome it and confess to being stimulated by it. Pitching *the right level of challenge* so as to provoke thinking and engagement in the student – without resulting in a sense of being overwhelmed – is what *a teacher's challenge* is largely about!

The following incident (recounted by another teacher) however seems to be the best indicator of their feeling for the subject: the students spent a two-night train journey, as part of their yearly excursion, single-mindedly – with obvious absorption and enjoyment – trying to crack a math puzzle that Gopi had given them at the start of the trip!

Appendix

Error Analysis Worksheet for Grade VIII

Q1.   Add 526 and 1378.

Q2.   Simplify: 56 – 85 + 37 – 96

Q3.   Add 3.75 and 13.

Q4.   Add –756 and 368.

Q5.   Write the number for: Five crore five lakh five thousand and fifty

Q6.   Subtract: 2003 – 678

Q7.   Subtract 657 from –425.

Q8.   Subtract –463 from –528.

Q9.   Subtract 6.45 from 14.

Q10.   Subtract 675 from 236.

Q11.   Multiply: 67×9

Q12.   Multiply: 64×42

Q13.   Multiply: 300×1000

Q14.   Multiply: 3.5×2.6

Q15.   Multiply $(-12) \times (-34)$

Q16.   Divide 636 by 6.

Q17.   Divide 720 by 9.

Q18.   Divide 3201 by 3.

Q19.   Divide 6000 by 200.

Q20.   Divide 4200 by 7.

3

TWO WRONGS CAN MAKE A RIGHT

The significance of a student being comfortable (if not fluent) with the medium of communication cannot be overstated. Howsoever sound a student's grasp of any subject may be, learning is not deemed complete until the learner's understanding can be clearly articulated. Whether it is answering a given question, or framing one's doubts clearly for the teacher to answer, the skill of clearly expressing oneself in the medium of instruction is of vital importance. When this medium is a foreign tongue like English – as it is in many Indian schools – English language teachers across the country face an enormous challenge as they strive to develop the reading and writing skills of their students.

This chapter describes one English teacher's mode of engagement with his students as part of the Reflective Learner Programme. It not only elaborates his efforts to study their error patterns, by gathering data, but also describes the consequently observed shifts in the quality of their writing. More importantly, it highlights perceptible changes in their attitudes to writing and their enhanced interest in the English language. It ends on a reflective note, bringing to the fore the teacher's takeaways and the significance of the onward journey for all: the teacher as well as the taught.

The Teacher-Researcher

At the time of conducting this action research, Michael Moses was teaching English to Grade VIII at Taktse International School, Sikkim. In 2016, over a period of four months, he participated in the Reflective Learner Programme by connecting with the facilitator (located in Bangalore) every week over Skype and email.

For some time, Michael had become interested in addressing the challenges that some of his students were facing in expressing themselves clearly and correctly in English. In the academic session 2016-17, when he took on Grade VIII as an English teacher, he was especially keen to build the language skills of his eighth

> Thanks for your note. I was really struck by your observation that it is primarily the identification of errors that students need to be taught, even before we get into finding strategies for them to address these errors. Wonderful start, Michael!
>
> - Email from the facilitator to Michael

graders so that they would not be burdened at least by the fundamental issues, particularly in the near future while preparing for the Board Exam in Grade X. Finally, his need to overcome these challenges took on a concrete form when he embarked on the Reflective Learner Programme in 2016.

Beginning with the identification of five students in his class who, he felt, were struggling to write correctly, Michael worked his way systematically through a stepwise process of action research that was aimed at developing the reflective learner in them. From time to time, he expanded his efforts to include the entire class, especially when he felt the exercise would benefit all learners, or when he wished to avoid drawing special attention to the struggles of these five students. In addition, he confronted the challenge to continuously focus on the goals of the action research, which demanded that he consistently keep track of the five students and make periodic notes on their progress.

Preparing the Ground

In the academic year 2016-2017, Michael identified five students in Grade VIII who, he felt, were struggling to write correctly. He then began his action research by observing the most common errors made by these five students, with the aim of getting them to fix these errors. No sooner had he started, than he realised that the students primarily needed to be taught *the identification of errors*, even before setting out to find strategies to address these errors. In other words, Michael saw the need for the students to *first see that something was amiss*. So, he set about devising ways of getting them sensitised in this direction.

Thank you for today's meeting. Here's what we discussed.

1) Select a common recurring error for the individual students.

2) Develop strategies to help them find the errors.

3) Reading as a strategy to find errors with pointers for what to look for.

4) At a later stage, find strategies to solve the errors.

5) Scan a copy of students' work and email it.

- Email from Michael to the facilitator in the 1st week of the programme

Michael anticipated (and later experienced) a resistance in the students' minds to spotting errors. So, he toyed with the idea of having them note the number of times they got something *right*. As already mentioned in Chapter 1, Taktse International School has in place a practice wherein students proofread their own work and mark the errors in green ink (see Figure 1), before turning it in. Thus, Michael could see that it wouldn't be a totally new exercise for them.

However, he felt that students were often unclear as to *what to look for*, when they were simply told to proofread their work. Therefore, he planned to give them a checklist of errors to look out for (see Table 1). He felt that in scanning one specific error at a time, they would be more likely to catch their errors.

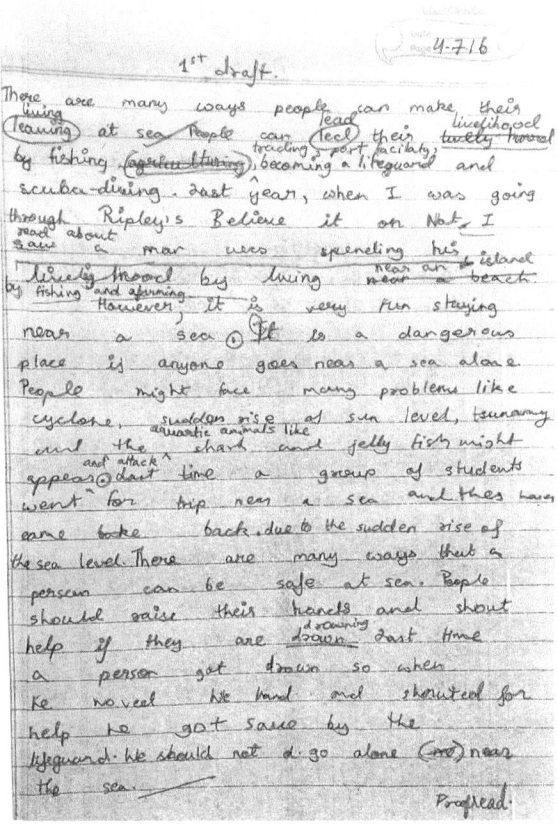

Figure 1: Proofread sample by a student

During their weekly call, the facilitator posed the following two apprehensions about this exercise:

1. Would the students find it to be too much of a burden?
2. How would he know that they were not getting put off by this demand for extra effort?

In response to the first question, Michael hoped that they would do the exercise in a stepwise manner, and not in their usual manner of looking for *all* errors *at the same time.*

As for the second, he noted that the quality of the students' work would reflect their state of mind: in other words, if he discerned that their work had been done randomly, without having been closely examined, he would (to an extent) assume that they might be getting put off. At the same time, he also felt that doing this exercise for the entire class would be useful, too, as the brighter students would surely benefit from it. For instance, he had earlier tried the same with descriptive writing by making a checklist of the important elements that should be included in their writing. They had to satisfy these requirements as they wrote out the passage. This was, by his own admission, a tough exercise, but one which the brighter students felt made their writing better. Unfortunately, the weaker ones could not cope. (Michael's labelling of students as 'brighter' and 'weaker' also underwent a change through this research, as explained in a later section.)

Arriving at a Workable Strategy

Michael drew up the checklist shown in Table 1 to serve as a guide for all his students (not only the five struggling ones) to spot different types of 'correct' entries in their English writing. Against each item in the checklist, he asked students to enter the number of such 'correct' elements in their writing. Michael thought of focusing on the usage of articles, to begin with, and he planned to check the numbers entered by students with their actual work in order to see if they had filled it in correctly.

Table 1: A checklist

S. no.	Checklist item
1	Clear sentences
2	Verbs used in the correct form and place
3	Singular nouns have singular verbs.
4	Plural nouns have plural verbs
5	Tenses used correctly
6	Correct usage of articles 'a', 'an' and 'the'
7	Correct Usage of Prepositions
8	Sentences end with the appropriate punctuation marks
9	Correct usage of commas
10	Usage of appropriate vocabulary

Not surprisingly, (after a week of administering this exercise) he reverted with the finding that students had experienced difficulty filling the checklist. It was a learning experience for him as he realised that expecting the students to complete the entire checklist was asking too much of them. And that perhaps he should narrow the checklist down to *one thing at a time*. It also occurred to him that the same checklist may not work for everyone, and that he could consider focusing on punctuation, articles or prepositions with only the five struggling students, who certainly needed an intervention of this sort. Michael also realised, through this exercise, that his students needed reinforcement in understanding what really is meant, say, by a 'clear sentence'. He also began

I find it so exciting when they are able to spot their own errors. I have told them to correct their errors in a different colour ink. I just write in the margin - indicating the errors. When a girl came up and said she had not understood punctuation, I found that she understood it after I showed her just two samples and began writing in the margin. She is, however, a capable girl.

– Michael, in a chat with the facilitator, 6 weeks after embarking on this research

thinking about finer details like sequencing, i.e. which of these items he should ask the students to focus on first: he thought of beginning with a checklist item that *they were already confident about,* so that they felt reassured.

By the fifth week of the programme, Michael found out that his students were excited about weeding out one error at a time. He began by asking all the students to focus on simple punctuation first: comma, exclamation mark, etc. They began by working on short pieces of written work: he told them to first copy down different dialogues from a given text, so as to get a sense of where, for instance, quotation marks appeared. Once they got the sense, they then had to write five dialogues on their own. At the end, they had to rate their work on a scale of 1 to 10[1].

Michael acknowledged that this was a better route than counting the number of errors. As can be seen, Michael had, by now, also factored into his strategy a concern for the inclusion of all students. The main reason for expanding the scope of the exercise, to deliberately include the entire class, was to prevent the five 'struggling' students from feeling lesser. Students were divided into groups of five – just to camouflage the intent of helping the struggling students. In fact, the exercise was benefiting the advanced students as well, as they, too, seldom proofread their work properly; and this ensured that they didn't forget to insert, say, commas at the right place. When he felt that a particular student did not need help in the usage of articles, for instance, he gave him/her another item from the checklist to explore. Thus, everyone got some kind of work – so no one would feel lesser or greater. Also, he began giving some optional homework, in addition to regular homework, and asked them to rate themselves on punctuation at the end of every piece of work.

Within a short time span of implementing this exercise, Michael already noticed a significant improvement in the written work of one of the students (which was confirmed by the appreciative call

---

[1] Student rating scale: 1, 2, 3 – needs improvement; 4, 5 – average; 6, 7 – good; 8, 9 – very good; and 10 – excellent.

that he received from his parents). Moreover, in demanding a critical evaluation of the work from the student, Michael had begun shifting the onus of rating the work from teacher to student. A concern for quality of work was thus being shared by both the teacher and the student through this exercise.

Stepping up the Pace

In the sixth week, Michael felt the need to change gear. He still wanted to focus on weeding out one error at a time, but exams were just a month and fifteen days away – too short an interval to get the students to conquer their errors *one at a time*. So, he adopted the strategy of noting the type of error (e.g. prepositional or article error) in the margin, *without indicating its exact location.* Given the crucial juncture, he felt this would be more concrete than students just proofreading their own work. Moreover, identifying the location of the cited error also helped in posing a challenge to each student.

> Prior to this, I would spoon-feed the students with the correct spellings, verbs, tenses, etc.
>
> Now, I simply give a hint with a pointer in the margin. The onus is on the student to find and fix the error – this challenges the student – at the same time, they get sufficient guidance as to what the error may be.
>
> – Michael's notes, 6 weeks after embarking on this research

Further, it panned out that as the teacher began to enjoy this new way of correcting the students' work, so did the students. While it was initially a challenge for Michael, he noted that he slowly got better at pinpointing the exact nature of the error; and students, too, began to feel excited that they could spot as well as fix their own errors. Consequently, Michael began to need less and less time to carry out this style of correction.

Figures 2 and 3 are samples of Michael's mode of correcting notebooks prior to and after embarking on this programme, respectively. Figure 2 shows how the teacher has clearly shown each error at its exact location. Figure 3 illustrates *indications given by the teacher, in the margin,* of a nearby error – so that the *student is compelled to think* about the exact location of this error. Michael noted that in the past he explicitly pointed out even minor errors like punctuation and spellings to the students, thus giving them no room to spot and correct their own errors. He realised that his earlier method of correction was not empowering, as the students did not feel the need to observe their work or reflect on it.

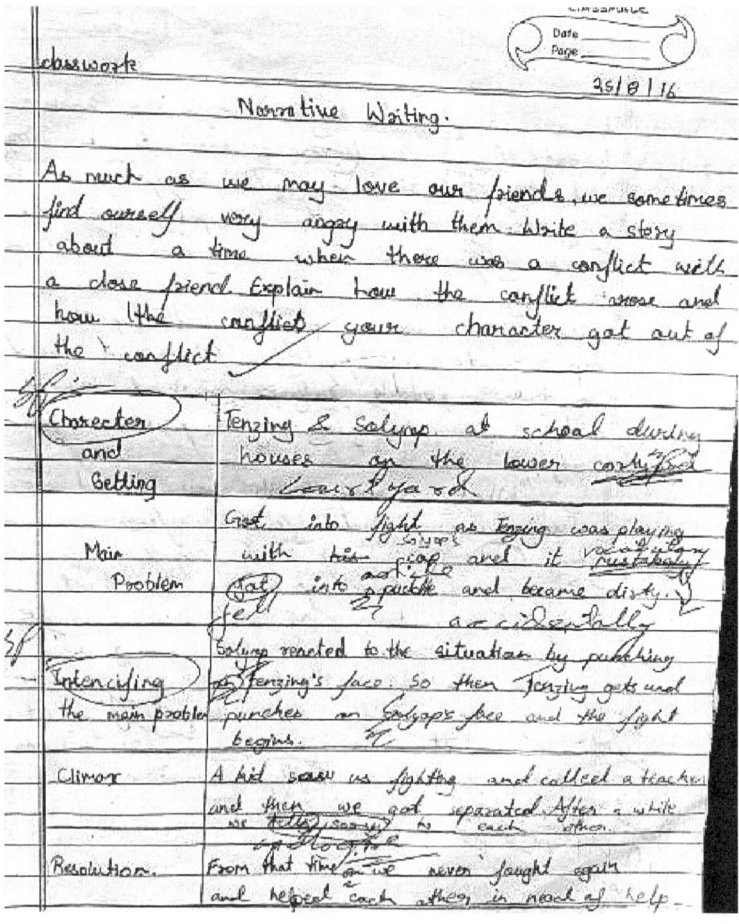

Figure 2: Old method of correction

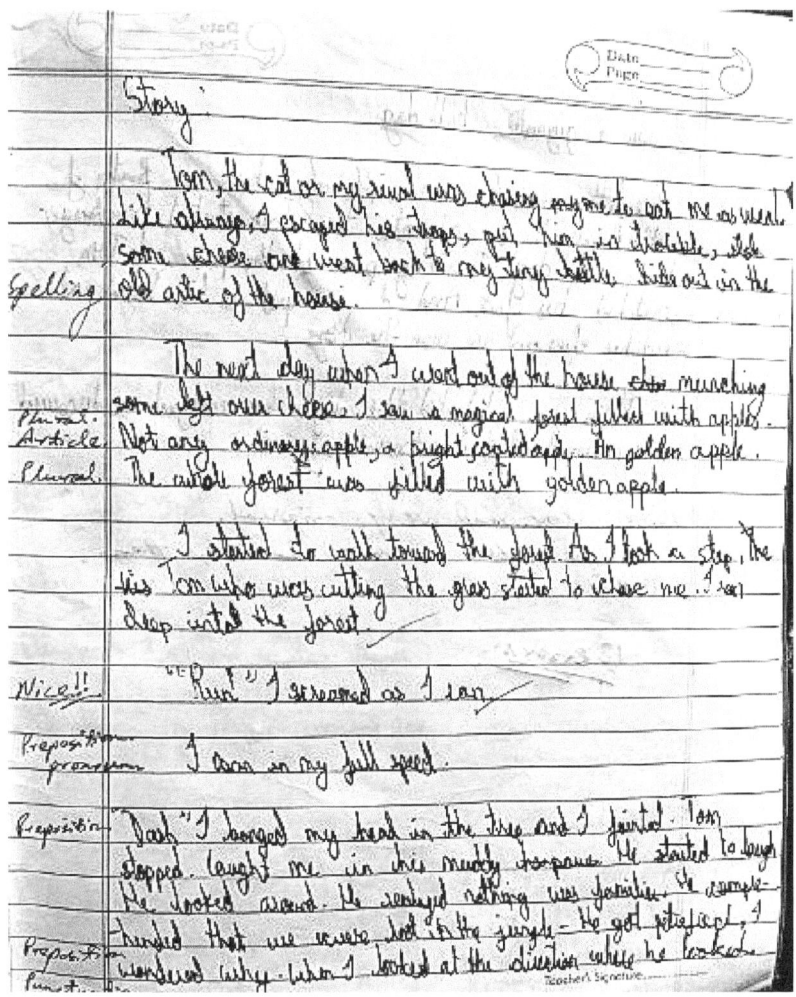

Figure 3: New method of error indication

Implementing the Chosen Strategy

Having arrived at the new error correction strategy (introduced in the previous section), Michael took the decision to sustain its usage for the next few weeks so as to really test out its efficacy. It had taken him six weeks to zero in on this as an effective method, and so he now felt the need to give it time to work.

Along with marking the indications for the whole class through the new strategy, Michael wanted to focus on the five struggling students to see if they could spot the exact location of the indicated error. Initially, he tried sitting with them in pairs but soon found that they needed one-on-one sessions, without which the exercise was rendered ineffective. Therefore, over the next few weeks, Michael began investing one-on-one time with each of the five struggling students, with the intention of getting them to first understand *why* something was an error. (Michael observed that the exercise in turn was helping him do his job better, too: his corrections were becoming more detailed and focused.)

For instance, in the case of Abhijit[2], Michael scaffolded the process by allowing the

> Michael: They said this is challenging them more. May not be true for every student, but those who are self-aware are finding it useful.
>
> Facilitator: How are your 5 struggling students finding this new way of correction?
>
> Michael: One is not comfortable; I need to sit with him. Two have mixed reactions, and the other two are very excited. I need to make the time to sit with those who are not comfortable and help them with this. Am I spoon-feeding?
>
> Facilitator: The best way for you to know that is to ask yourself whether they would spot the error without your doing this for them.
>
> Michael: No, they would not spot it by themselves. If I give them support by mentioning it in the margin, I feel they will be able to identify the error more easily.
>
> - An excerpt from a discussion between Michael and the facilitator during the 7th week

student to figure out how he had used an incorrect preposition. Slowly and systematically, Michael led Abhijit through a process of examining the usage of prepositions in different instances. For example, when Abhijit wrote 'standing in the gate', Michael first used a dictionary to show him a list of prepositions. He then asked Abhijit

[2] All student names have been changed in order to preserve confidentiality.

if 'standing in the gate' was correct. 'Yes,' was the student's pat reply. Not wanting to correct him right away, Michael drew his attention to where he was right now. 'In the class,' came Abhijit's prompt response. Continuing thus, Abhijit admitted he was sitting *on* the chair *in* the class. Finally, he was able to re-examine if he was *inside* the gate; and realised that a better preposition in this phrase would be 'near' – standing *near* the gate. Michael observed that Abhijit felt empowered at the end of the process.

With Lakshman, he also adopted a read-aloud strategy in addition to the new correction method: this student read aloud his work to guess where he may have gone wrong. For example, upon repeating the phrase 'drive the plane' a few times – and with Michael nudging him to think about what one does with a plane – the student suddenly realised that one *flies* a plane, not *drives* it.

Interestingly, within a week of adopting the new strategy, Michael found that two of the students – Lakshman and Krishna – were able to correct their errors just by seeing the teacher's indications in the margin. They seemed to enjoy the empowerment of spotting and fixing their own errors. Moreover, like Lakshman, Anil could spot and fix his errors merely by reading aloud his work.

Further, Michael noticed that Lakshman's errors in his written work were quite simple, and mostly occurred because he did not proofread his work after writing and was in a hurry to just complete his work and turn it in. But more significantly, once Lakshman saw that he could fix the errors on his own, he became more confident and began taking a greater interest in writing.

Michael adopted a phased method of correction. First, the student was encouraged to revisit his own work and make corrections as he deemed fit. This was then followed by Michael going through the work and inserting notes in the margin that indicated (but did not clearly pinpoint) further corrections that were needed. Finally, the student reviewed the work by acting on the indications given by Michael.

Figure 4 is a sample of this sequence of corrections in Lakshman's work – the notes in the margin have been inserted by Michael, and the corrections in the body of the text by the student. (Insertions in the circles were made by the student *before* the teacher corrected his work, while the other changes in the text were inserted *after* taking a cue from the teacher's notes in the margin.)

In this manner, he began enabling the students to figure out the kinds of errors that they had made. Michael noted that his altered correction method, along with the specific strategies for the struggling students, provided them with the opportunity to reflect on their work. He began to see the value in this – and slowly, so did his students.

Error Patterns

As the research progressed, Michael began to see a pattern in the errors made. Across students, he noted that the commonest errors were in prepositions, spellings and punctuation. The rarest errors were adjectives, adverbs, conjunctions, and an error that Michael coined as PATS (when to change the paragraphs, i.e. Place, Action, Time and Speech or speaker) and syntax errors. He found that students quickly got rid of prepositional, article and punctuation errors. The errors that they found difficult to conquer, however, varied from student to student. The reason behind their struggle could vary from reasons such as their standard of English being below the required grade level, which, in turn, could be because the concept may not have been taught in a way that every student could grasp it. Perhaps some needed a reinforcement of the required concept so that they could understand it better. In some cases, it could even be because the student simply did not know that it was an error.

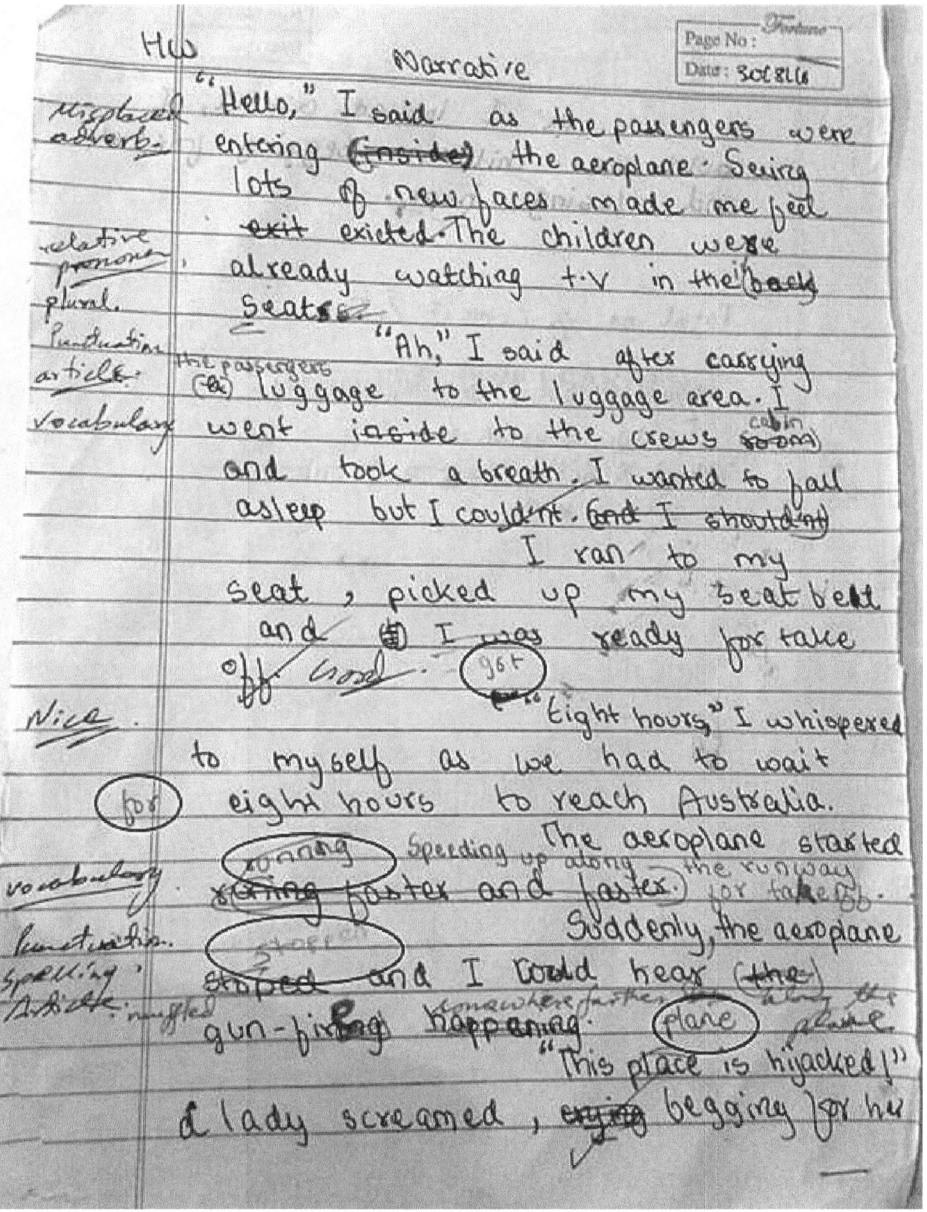

Figure 4: Sample of Lakshman's work

Time Management

In a study such as this, the constraint of time has to be routinely assessed and managed efficiently. And since Michael had to work on lesson plans, correction, routine documentation, etc. in addition to this action research, he prioritised his tasks by correcting the work of the most-needy students first. Then he corrected the day scholars' work, and finally the boarders' assignments, as he could work on the latter even after school hours –

> I take approximately 15-25 minutes to correct and make notes in a student's notebook. It depends on the kind of writing, with narratives and articles taking the most time. Dialogues and sentence exercises take 8-10 minutes each. Also, the complexity of errors sometimes demands more time and analysis before I write a comment.
>
> – *Email from Michael to the facilitator in the 7th week*

being a campus resident himself. He however ensured that not a single student's work was left uncorrected. Michael thus arrived at an optimal way of managing time. While he had to spend 30 to 40 minutes per notebook at the start, within a couple of weeks this investment of time dropped to an average of seven minutes per notebook, with some exceptions (described in his email to the facilitator in the seventh week; see box alongside).

Shifts in Students' Attitudes and Work

In the eighth week, Michael noted that the aforementioned five students (who were the focus of his action research) were noticeably more aware of their errors and were investing the effort to fix them. He observed this trend particularly after conducting a Mock Quiz on a Monday as well as the following Wednesday. All the five students did badly on Monday, but reasonably well on Wednesday. Michael identified the cause for this shift in performance to be his marking scheme: In the Monday Quiz, he did not mark the errors in the margin (as he had been doing so far), which turned out to be a premature decision. Barring one of them, none of the students diagnosed exactly where they had made the errors that Michael had just indicated as a total number. So, for the Wednesday Quiz, Michael went back to his usual practice of indicating the errors in the margin, which then had to be spotted and corrected by the students. Only after they had done so, did Michael announce the total marks. Amazingly, now *all five of them were able to fix their errors* with Michael prompting them.

By the ninth week, Michael noted a substantive decrease in the number of errors made by these five students: Anil was able to fix 70 percent of his errors; and Lakshman went from making 27 errors to 15. (Lakshman could spot and correct errors with the help of pointers as well as by reading his work aloud.) Krishna and Abhijit, who had initially found writing challenging, began to show more interest in written work. (And even though the number of errors in both their work increased, they were able to use dialogues, complex sentences, metaphors, similes and enhanced vocabulary with more confidence. Also, both of them could spot and fix most of the errors in their work.) Pritam's exposure to English was not as much as the others, hence his progress did not manifest as a decreasing number of errors. However, he showed an enhancement in vocabulary and an increased confidence to attempt writing complex sentences, by the end of the research. In all, Lakshman and Anil made the fastest progress, while Krishna had a personal preference to verbally diagnosing his errors, rather than writing it out!

Keeping this shift in mind, and on the suggestion of the facilitator, Michael asked the five students to make a table of their shift in errors, category wise, so that they could get a sense of ownership of their progress. Table 2 shows two such samples.

Table 2: Shift in the number of errors

	Name: Anil			Name: Abhijit		
Date	Aug 30	Sep 16	Oct 5	Sep 8	Sep 21	Oct 5
Type of error	Number of errors			Number of errors		
Adjective			2	1		5
Adverb	3					
Articles	3	2	3	1		2
Capitalisation	1	1	1			
Clarity		1	1			1
Conjunction						1
Noun						
Legibility						
Plural	1		2	1		3
Preposition		1		4	3	1
Pronoun	1	2			1	5
Punctuation	3	3	1		7	2
Spelling	2	4		1		2
Syntax/REALISM	1		1			2
Tense					2	1
Verb	2	2	4	3	1	
Vocabulary	8	2			1	2
Repetition/SYNTAX	2	2		1		
Numeric						
PATS[3]		2				
Incomplete sentence					1	0
Total	27	22	15	12	16	27

Further, Michael drew up a three-month timeline to compare the errors made by each of the five students over three of the four months that he had carried out his study.

---

[3] PATS: Michael coined this abbreviation to indicate errors that involved attention to changing paragraphs so as to indicate a change in Place, Action, Time or Speech. Paragraphs in a narrative are supposed to change when any of these or a combination of these change.

In an attempt to study trends, he drew a graph of Krishna's errors. As can be seen from Figure 5, some errors decreased in frequency from August to October (usage of articles, plural form and vocabulary) while certain others (spellings) increased. Michael attributed the increased spelling errors to Krishna's enhanced vocabulary, and this was another instance of his seeing errors in a nuanced manner. It was finer observations such as these that led to a change in the way Michael viewed his students: as not necessarily being 'bright' or 'weak' but as merely struggling to master the skills of writing.

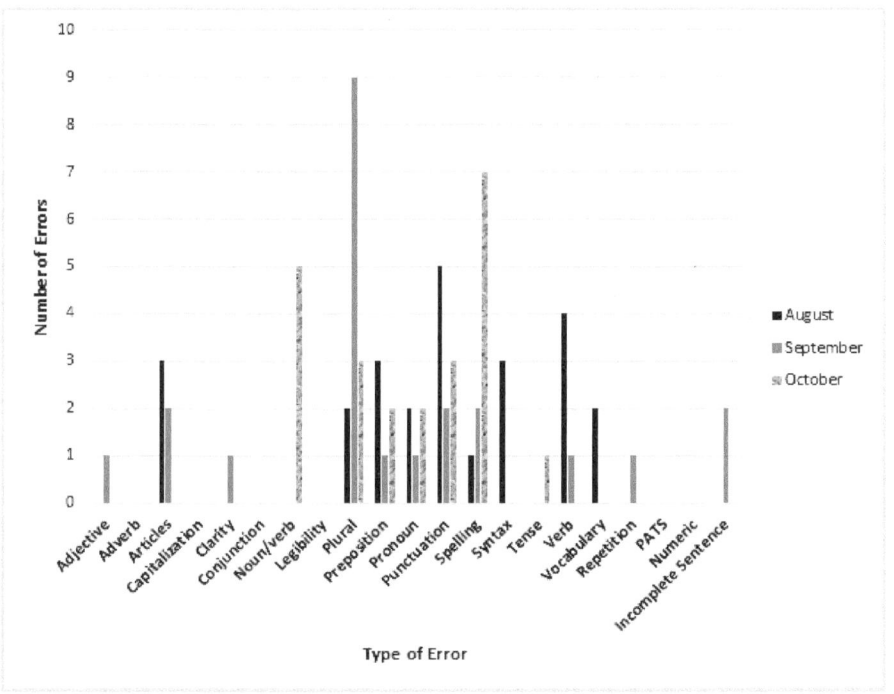

Figure 5: Frequency of errors over three months

Michael reviewed the work of the five struggling students both at the start and at the end of the programme, and observed that they had become better at spotting and fixing indicated errors without his intervention: he was able to see visible shifts in all of them. While these students had initially needed one-on-one guidance from the teacher to fix the indicated errors, he was elated that in just a short time span of four months the 'strugglers' had quickly taken over this task on their own. Of the five, Michael found that Abhijit, Anil and Lakshman had moved forward significantly in this regard.

Figures 6 and 7 show two samples of Krishna's work at the start and end of the programme, respectively. As before, the notes in the margin are made by the teacher, while all the changes in the body of the text are by the student. Again, insertions in the circles were made by the student *before* the teacher corrected his work, while the other changes in the text were inserted *after* taking a cue from the teacher's notes in the margin. The insertions of the latter type are conspicuous by their absence in Figure 6. Figure 6 thus shows several indications by the teacher which the student has *not managed to address* (syntax, vocabulary, punctuation, plural form), while Figure 7 shows progress in this regard. Acting on the indications made by the teacher therefore took some time. In three months, Krishna shows clear progress in terms of mastery over verb tense errors, use of specific vocabulary and syntax. The number of punctuation errors has gone down by 50 per cent. Overall the shift is from 12 errors to 10, as the student's spelling errors went up as a result of playing with new words like 'halted' and 'thump'.

Figures 8, 9 and 10 are end-of-programme samples of Lakshman's, Anil's and Abhijit's work, respectively. Figure 8 shows that Lakshman has managed to address every error indicated by his teacher: other than a punctuation and syntax error, as opposed to his struggle to even identify that he had made an error when he initially began the programme. Figure 9 shows how Anil has correctly managed to fix 100 per cent of his errors with the help of the pointers in the margin.

Initially, Anil would have few errors that he could not spot or that he would be unable to fix, but at the end of the three months, he could fix every error with the help of pointers. From Figure 10, it is evident that Abhijit managed to go from not knowing what his errors were to finally managing to correct 100 per cent of his errors – with the help of pointers. His errors were basically recurring errors like a repeated (and incorrect) use of 'all'. Abhijit also learnt how to correct his vocabulary errors by thinking of simpler words.

Pritam was the only student who did not show visible progress in reducing the number of errors. But Michael could see a clear improvement in the quality of his work both from the point of view of vocabulary (which increased) and his sentences which moved from simple to complex.

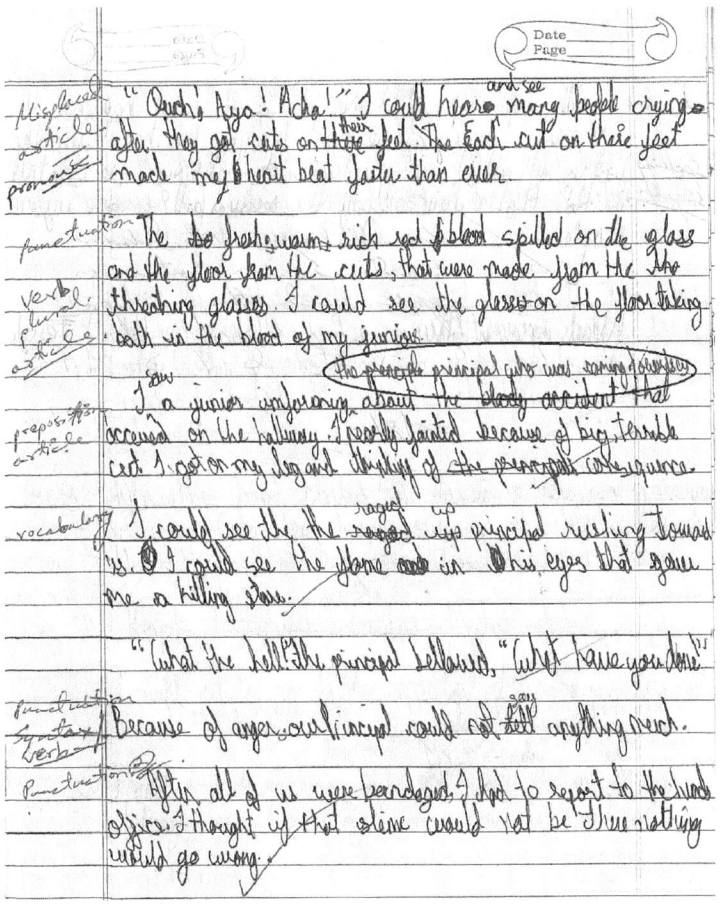

Figure 6: Sample of Krishna's work at the start of the programme

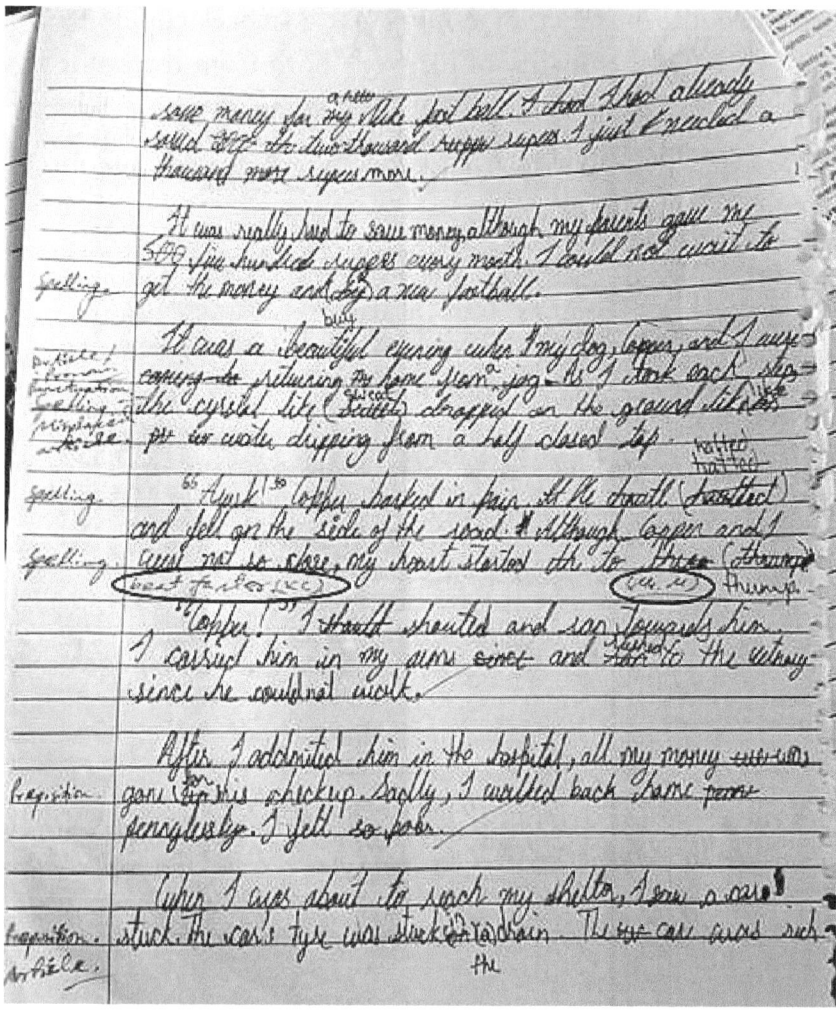

Figure 7: Sample of Krishna's work at the end of the programme

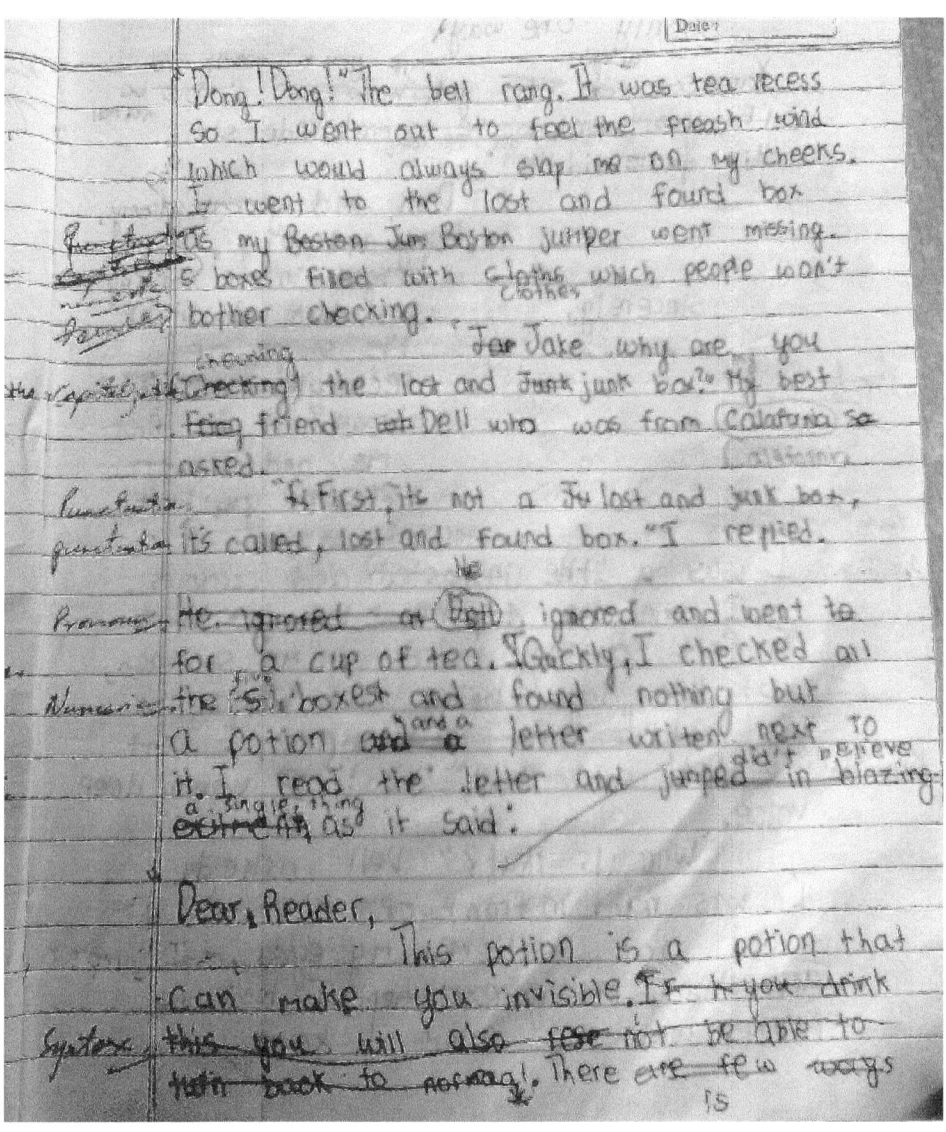

Figure 8: Sample of Lakshman's work

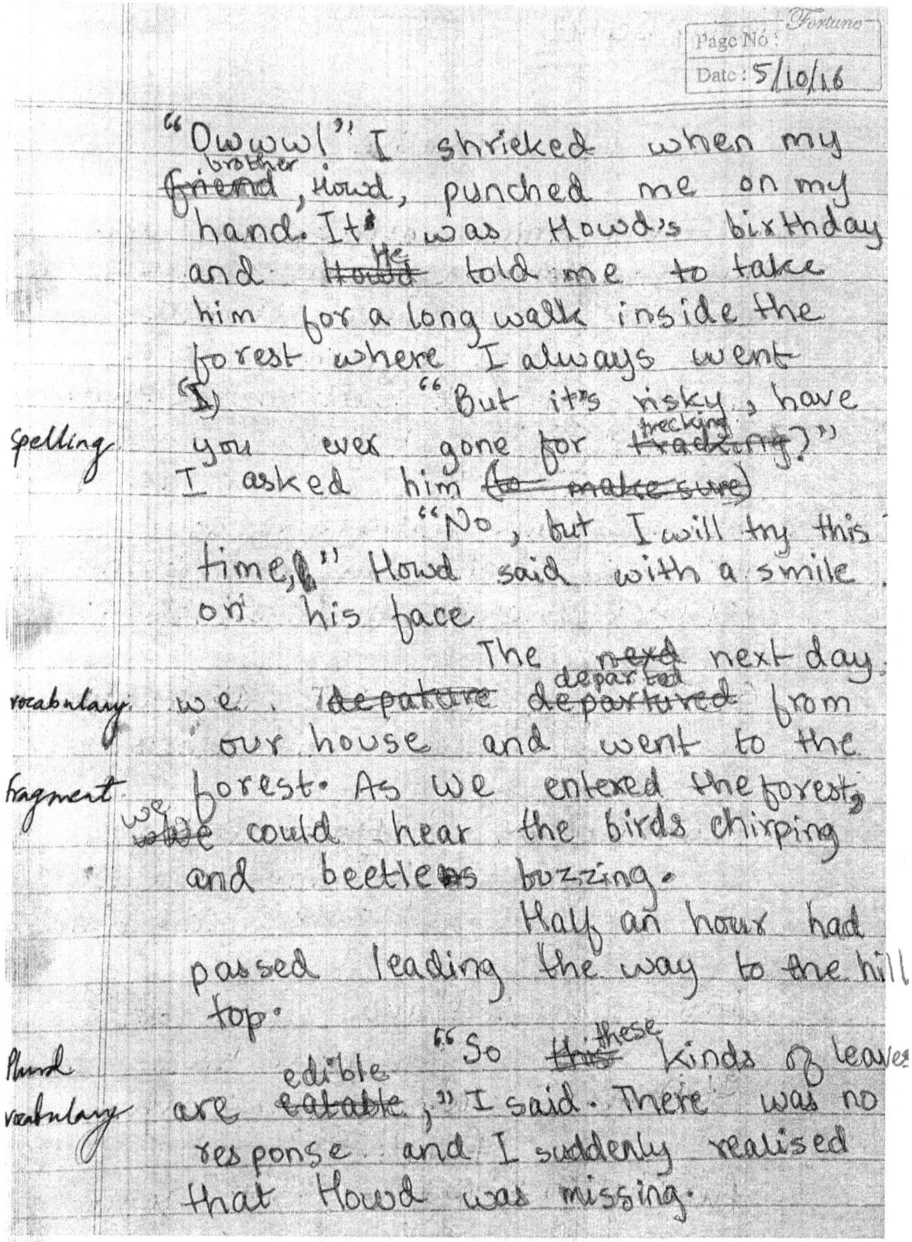

Page No:
Date: 5/10/16

"Owwwl" I shrieked when my ~~friend~~ brother, Howd, punched me on my hand. It was Howd's birthday and ~~Howd~~ He told me to take him for a long walk inside the forest where I always went.

"But it's risky, have you ever gone for ~~tracking~~ trecking?" I asked him ~~(to make sure)~~

"No, but I will try this time," Howd said with a smile on his face.

The ~~next~~ next day we ~~depature~~ ~~departured~~ departed from our house and went to the forest. As we entered the forest, ~~whe~~ we could hear the birds chirping and beetles buzzing.

Half an hour had passed leading the way to the hill top.

"So ~~this~~ these kinds of leaves are ~~eatable~~ edible," I said. There was no response and I suddenly realised that Howd was missing.

spelling

vocabulary

fragment

Plural

vocabulary

Figure 9: Sample of Anil's work

Margin annotations (left): misplaced, adjective, tense, Syntax, Adjective, pronoun, plural, Spelling, vocabulary, article, Punctuation, adjective, pronoun, Punctuation, Article, Preposition, vocabulary, Article, vocabs, Plural, conjunction, spelling, Spelling, pronoun

Last year, when I got my new phone, I was getting disgusting and dirty day by day as I was always ingrossed in my phone. I started to eat (~~all~~) unhealthy food and I didn't care(d) about what I am doing. These days some people are (~~effecting~~) damaging their body very badly by eating (~~all those~~) unhealthy food and not ~~munching~~ excersing at all.

Eating healthy food is the main idea how we can maintain our body as we spoil our body by eating (~~all those~~) junk and unhealthy food. The other name for unhealthy food will be oily foods which make you fat if you take (~~unlimitedly~~) carelessly. These oily foods have (~~to~~) lots of colesterol which will block our heart and may lead to heart attack. Before, when I used to eat (~~all those~~) unhealthy items, I was unable to run, but (~~now~~) after I stopped touching those junks, (~~to~~) I can run at a great speed.

We should have the habit of keeping our surroundings and belongings clean which will (~~under~~) have a positive effect in our body. Unclean clothes and places attract the different kinds of illness and some insects with it. Insects like mosquitoes and flies are very disgusting and they are attracted by the unclean clothes and dirty places and then they spread out the disease called (~~dengue~~) dengu). Keeping our homes clean also matters as in our house also many illness spread when it is not clean, so this will also help us in keeping our body healthy.

Figure 10: Sample of Abhijit's work

Students' Feedback

At the end of the programme, the facilitator spoke to the entire Grade VIII over a Skype call to find out their responses to Michael's changed method of correction. Students said that they found the new method to be useful, but also acknowledged that correcting their own mistakes proved to be a huge challenge at first. Some of them also felt that the resulting awareness about their own mistakes had equipped them better to prepare for the International General Certificate of Secondary Education (IGCSE)[4] Board Exam in the next couple of years, where they could not afford to make punctuation and grammatical mistakes. In a class of 23 students, 10 admitted to feeling bored with English writing at the start of the study, but by the end, half this number (five) continued to feel bored. Two students confessed that their interest depended on their mood.

Michael's core study group of five students gave him written feedback; they were also interviewed by the facilitator to gauge their takeaway. Their responses have been summarised as follows:

1. Krishna admitted that he had now become more aware of the sorts of mistakes that he tended to make, and therefore did not repeat the same mistakes. He also admitted candidly: 'My writing used to be very mood dependent. It is less so now. I like writing narratives nowadays.'

2. Abhijit rated himself before the programme as 'a moderate writer who was scared of writing', but now saw himself as 'a good writer who had started using complex sentences'. He attributed this shift to the gain in his confidence because of correcting his own mistakes: 'I realised that the mistakes I was making were all silly and careless.' More importantly, he acknowledged moving from being scared at the thought of writing to now feeling excited about it.

---

[4] IGCSE is a globally recognised qualification, taken at the Grade 10 level, similar to the Grade 10 examinations of the Central Board of Secondary Education (CBSE) and Indian Certificate of Secondary Education (ICSE) or the Middle Years Programme of the International Baccalaureate (IB).

3. Pritam saw himself moving from being a 'bad writer' before the programme to now being a 'moderate writer'. He attributed this shift to a heightened level of concentration in class, and acknowledged moving from being 'scared of writing' to feeling confident enough to tackle writing tasks quickly and with enjoyment.

4. From starting off as a bored student who had no interest in writing, Anil now declared: 'The quality of my work is completely different in these past few months. I enjoy writing my own stories and realised how creative I am.' Like Pritam, he, too, admitted that his interest grew as he began to focus more.

5. Lakshman said: 'In the beginning of the programme, Mr Michael corrected my punctuation and grammar in a way that I found very useful, as I could recognise my own mistakes; and I really feel that I have improved a lot as a result.' He, too, acknowledged that he had turned into an interested and confident writer from being a bored and diffident one. He pronounced, with pride: 'My boredom has vanished!'

Teacher's Observations of Student Shifts

By the end of the programme, Michael drew the following specific and general conclusions about the student sample that he had focused on:

1. Amongst the five most 'struggling' students, Anil and Lakshman have moved out of the struggling category.

2. As of now, Abhijit, Anil and Lakshman can fix most of the errors with minimum guidance, especially when they read aloud their work.

3. There is a noticeable change in the time taken by Lakshman to get into a task and to complete it. There is greater readiness and interest.

4. Krishna is a reluctant, not a struggling, student. He can spot and correct all his errors when he reads his work aloud. However, he is still not motivated to do it on his own, even though he corrects his errors verbally. It all depends on his mood.

5. Pritam has become a more confident writer even though he still makes a lot of grammatical errors.

6. Students are now aware of the common (yet crucial) errors that they make, from the pointers in the margin, which they see decreasing in number as they make progress.

7. Although students continue to make errors, when they re-check, they find and fix the errors with greater ease, as compared to before the programme.

8. The errors that the students make may change as they make efforts to improve. That, in itself, is an indicator of their becoming more skilled as well as more reflective – as they are now experimenting with complex forms of writing.

9. Most importantly, the students are now aware of their errors and have also been given strategies to find and fix them.

10. Students gained critical thinking skills while rating themselves on the quality of their own work.

11. The overall confidence levels of students increased noticeably.

Moving beyond Right and Wrong: Teacher's Takeaway

Before participating in the programme, Michael admits that he would have quite consciously labelled students as 'brighter' and 'weaker', but as he embarked on this research, he realised that these students were not weak. They were just struggling! The reasons, he deciphered, were many: lack of motivation, state of mind, repeatedly being told that they never get things right and so on. He can now see that although he would regularly give extra help and support to those who were struggling, it never occurred to him to make a conscious effort to actually identify students' difficulties and design specific strategies to address them. The difference with such a programme was that he got an opportunity to look into his own mindset as well as the student's. As the action research progressed, he realised that the struggling students simply needed the push and motivation to move forward and learn, and this opened up avenues for them to confront their fears of writing and learning.

Towards the last stages of his action research, Michael made a significant discovery about his students' performance: while some errors such as omission or incorrect use of articles and prepositions decreased over the course of the programme (four months), others such as punctuation and spelling errors increased, as they were now trying to use more complex structures. Thus, Michael began to view errors in a more nuanced fashion – seeing that a larger number of errors does not necessarily imply poorer writing skills. On the contrary, he now recognised them as a sign of increased confidence in students, who felt emboldened to try writing complex sentences – where there is naturally more scope to make errors.

Some of Michael's other takeaways are as follows:

1. Before embarking on the Reflective Learner Programme, Michael would give general comments for overall improvement. But as a result of the programme, his specific indications really helped the students spot and fix their own errors.

2. Michael has also become more aware of grammatical concepts and competent in assisting students in a balanced way – that challenges them, even as it makes them capable of improving.

3. By changing the way that he corrected, Michael has been able to offer students the opportunity to reflect. (To him, the earlier correction method is akin to spoon-feeding the students with the correct spellings, verbs, tenses, etc.)

4. His new correction strategy has also allowed Michael to place the onus on students to find and fix the errors – challenging them, and at the same time, giving them sufficient guidance as to what the errors may be.

5. Michael has been motivated to explore new ways of learning (e.g. he has started regularly cross-checking the dictionary for spellings, correct usage, verbs, adverbs, adjectives, prepositions, etc. – initially, he found it challenging to swiftly spot or comment on these aspects.)

6. Michael also admits that his use of the English language is crisper now (he never learnt it technically and does not possess a degree in English).

7. He has become aware of and is able to acknowledge his assumptions about students (e.g. he identified his mistaken assumption about Krishna being a struggling student: he turned out to be a reluctant student, not a 'struggling' one.)

8. The programme has enabled him to encourage students who have been reluctant to invest efforts towards doing corrections to systematically find and correct their errors. (Some students found it burdensome to find and correct errors even a month into the programme, but finally relented.)

What Can an English Teacher Take Away from This Work?

Writing is not an easy skill to acquire; and on that account alone this is a very pertinent account of a teacher patiently leading students towards developing such a skill. It is not uncommon to find schools expecting students to acquire this skill as early as Grade II! Even in a school like Taktse International, where proofreading was a systemic expectation, it can be seen from this study that it was not *until the students themselves found value in this practice* that they began to do it *with attention*. This account of Michael's action research makes it evident that students can be motivated to undertake the journey of becoming more self-aware and focused – which, in turn, heightens the enjoyment of learning, in this case, mastering the skill of writing in English.

Further, each time some new learning happens, there is bound to be a spike in the number of errors; and it does take time for this to plateau or even drop down. All too often, parents and teachers forget this all-important principle, as they are blinded by their eagerness to see their children or students progress swiftly. The following are some valuable takeaways for English teachers:

1. The first and most powerful realisation is that a teacher's method of correction must give room to students for reflection. Unless this is done, there is little opportunity for the students to think about their own mistakes.

2. The altered method of correction enables the teacher to examine the students' work with greater care, as, for instance, Michael had to make detailed notes in the margin. Even the so-called 'advanced' students may need – and can therefore benefit from – this sort of correction.

3. This sort of action research can empower a teacher to become more efficient, as the teacher's competence in correcting students' work grows. (For instance, Michael invested an average of seven minutes per notebook by the end of the study, even as he made more precise notes in the margin about the type of error.)

4. Even as efficiency increases, the teacher will experience a demand to slow down and think before inserting a comment in the students' work – as a non-verbal conversation, so to speak, is triggered with the students. This sort of thoughtful exchange draws reciprocal responses from the students as well, as they, too, began to see the value in looking at their work with greater attention.

5. An investment of one-on-one time with the struggling students is necessary for some time – something that Michael needed to do less and less of, as the weeks slipped by.

6. A mere increase in the number of errors is no indication of deterioration in the quality of work. Instead, the usage of complex sentences by a student who was formerly only writing simple sentences shows a greater level of self-confidence, and of course, opens up the scope for making more errors.

The impact of this action research on the teacher is evident in at least one aspect: three years after starting this research, Michael continues to draw up his checklists which are a part of his classes at the start of every term. As the term rolls on, every now and then, he asks his students to actually count the number and types of errors that they make. He persists with this even though students occasionally find it difficult to identify the types of errors. He still regards mistakes as Missed Takes. Whether this research will have as consistent and sustained an impact on other aspects of his pedagogy remains to be seen.

CHAPTER

ERROR ANALYSIS AS AN EVALUATION TOOL

Kanchana Suryakumar

As a mathematics teacher, I was first introduced to the idea of 'error analysis' in 2015 by Dr Neeraja Raghavan, who was at that time facilitating an action research project for teachers transacting multi-age mathematics classes for middle school. I was struck by the powerful view that errors can open the window to discovering what a child has understood, rather than serve as a frustrating reminder to what a child hasn't understood.

Over time, my work in the area of error analysis has led me to see that a surprisingly simple – almost intuitive – idea such as this can actually cause a shift in perspective and classroom dynamics. It nudges the teacher towards becoming a student herself and coaxes a student to become a reflective thinker. This paper outlines one such journey that a group of students and two teachers (including myself) embarked upon. It captures the various strategies applied in the maths classroom, related successes and failures and the learning that resulted as we transitioned from analysing errors as an evaluation tool (for the teacher) to analysing them as a self-evaluation tool (for the student).

Introduction

This paper draws chiefly from the experience of two teachers – Hemalatha Gowda and I – who moved from the corporate world to the education sector, and have been teaching mathematics in both middle and high school at Poorna Learning Centre for 10 and 5 years, respectively. We have been actively involved in designing and implementing various strategies to make mathematics teaching and learning more meaningful and enjoyable. The classroom experiences referred to in this paper are specifically from my classroom, but both of us[1] were involved in discussing errors, ideating strategies and brainstorming the effectiveness of these strategies.

Research Environment

As mentioned earlier, this research was carried out in Poorna Learning Centre, which is an inclusive not-for-profit school located in the metropolitan city of Bangalore. The school has a refreshing attitude towards education, believing that education should be relevant, enjoyable and inclusive. It is a day school, with about 150 students, a maximum of 15 students per class, 30 teachers and support staff. The school has been supporting children from all socio-economic backgrounds, including first-generation learners – and 10 per cent of each grade comprises students with special needs.

Sample Group

The group whose work is referenced in this paper includes 14 students with whom we have worked for four years – Grades VII-X. Keeping their work in the seventh grade as a baseline, most of the examples and instances cited in this paper are from their work in the

---

[1] Throughout this paper, the use of the plural pronoun refers to the two teacher-researchers, viz. Hemalatha Gowda and myself.

ninth and tenth grades. The learning, both teachers' and students', is cumulative and spans three years (Grades VIII through X). This paper is an effort to document this three-year learning.

As is' the case in most classes, the children in this group have different levels of comfort with mathematics – some approach every problem purely as a pattern-matching or method-mapping exercise, while others have a deeper understanding of the subject and its application. Thus, each of them requires different levels of support – some require minimum guidance, while others require more in-class support or one-on-one assistance. The effort put in by the students, both in class and at home also varies – some are consistent workers, being diligent with their practice through the year, while others put in additional work only before a test or an examination.

The errors covered in the examples in this paper include those in arithmetic, algebra and geometry at the high-school level.

Background

Lockhart (2009) laments the current state of the mathematics curriculum and blames it for converting – what he believes to be – a form of art into something senseless and boring. He declares: 'If there is anything like a unifying aesthetic principle in mathematics, it is this: *simple is beautiful.*' He draws a distinction between emphasising the value of facts and appreciating the beauty of an idea. It is in the latter that he sees the possibility of triggering more ideas, thus allowing the learner to be released from the boundaries of reality so as to unleash creativity.

In our opinion, it is the disproportionate stress on facts and methods, in our mathematics curriculum, that has resulted in mistakes being looked upon more harshly than in other subjects. Even as failure and serendipity are discussed in encouraging (and even glorifying) terms in the other sciences, mathematics seems to have developed a reputation for expecting nothing short of perfection. While it is a lofty goal indeed to restore mathematics to its original beauty in a classroom, this research, nonetheless, attempts at least to make a start by helping students overcome their fear of errors.

Furthermore, moving away from the idea that errors in mathematics are typically 'careless' mistakes or a result of chance, Bouvier (1987) explains that these errors reflect how a student's mind has interpreted, understood and applied her learning in her *own* logical way. This places a demand on the teacher to attempt to transcend 'right' and 'wrong' and examine, instead, the thinking behind a mistake. This paper illustrates how we, as teacher-researchers, transitioned from pointing out errors in a student's work (in order to teach him how to avoid them), to analysing errors for a better understanding of the student's way of thinking. It also provides details on a subset of 'typical' errors seen and the strategies applied to observe, analyse and communicate these errors to the class. Moreover, the paper describes the attempts to help students analyse their own errors and our mutual learning in the process.

Error Analysis in the Mathematics Classroom

Over the course of this research, we discovered that the analysis of errors was sometimes more of an art than a science. It needed an environment that supported an open discussion of errors and a willingness to learn from (one's own as well as others') mistakes. It also required the creation and use of a simple glossary of terms that could help ease communication and convey ideas without confusion. This done, a space was then created for the discussion of strategies to overcome these errors.

The following sections discuss and detail out this process of error analysis in the classroom:

- ✦ Creating an environment for error analysis
- ✦ Categorising recurring errors
- ✦ Assigning errors to appropriate categories
- ✦ Implementing strategies to reduce recurring errors

Creating an environment for error analysis

Swartz (1976) argues that analysing mistakes and learning from them should be an important and integral part of the school curriculum.

He asserts the importance of implementing education policies that help teachers and students develop an attitude of enquiry towards mistakes, instead of looking down upon them or trying to hide them.

In the same spirit, the following processes and strategies – which developed organically over the years – were followed in the classroom to encourage students to get into a habit of analysing *their* understanding of a topic. Though captured in specific terms with specific outcomes for the purpose of documentation, the actual process involved trial and error, appropriate tweaks, discussions with students and brainstorming with other teachers. (The order in which they are listed in this paper do not necessarily reflect the order in which the strategies were actually tried.)

Self-assessment after every topic

At the end of a topic, a self-assessment form was provided to help students analyse how much they had understood and where they needed to go next. One class period was assigned for this purpose so that each student could 'take stock' of her own understanding of the topic just concluded. A sample self-assessment form is provided in Figure 1. The students had to choose and tick the column that best described their understanding of the topic. The sample problems helped them in this process. Once they were able to find the appropriate column, the column to its right would help them understand where they needed to go next.

Some students found it challenging to identify the column that matched their comfort level. The teacher spent some time asking these students leading questions (e.g. providing clues on how to solve a problem from that topic) that, in turn, helped them narrow down to the most appropriate column. Once the students filled the form, they would have one-on-one discussions with the teacher on strategies to reach the next level of understanding. Though the teacher provided this form, the goal was to get students to contribute to this template eventually.

Self-Assessment for Linear Equations in One Variable:

Topic	Understanding of the topic	Working with simple cases	High comfort-level and confidence with the topic
Linear Equation in one variable	I can differentiate between algebraic expressions and algebraic equations	I can identify linear equations of one, two or more variables	I can identify equations of a higher degree (e.g. quadratic, cubic)
Solving a given linear equation in one variable	I can solve a simple linear equation with one variable on one side of the equation e.g. $3x-5=10$	I can solve a linear equation with the same variable on both sides e.g $8x+4=3(x-1)+7$	I can solve a linear equation in one variable with fractional coefficients and fractional constants on both sides of the equation e.g. $x/2-1/5=(4x+3)/12$
Creating a linear equation in one variable, from given real-world situations	I can create a simple linear equation with one variable on one side of the equation e.g. 15 added to twice a number is 25	I can create a linear equation with linear expressions on both sides of the equation e.g. X's mother is six times X's current age. Five years from now, X will be one-third his mother's age. Find their current ages	I can create a linear equation to represent complex situations involving fractions. e.g. The denominator of a rational number is 8 more than its numerator. If the numerator is increased by 17 and the denominator is decreased by 1, the resulting number is 3/2. Find the rational number.

Additional Comments: (Please write a few lines about your experience with the topic, whether you need to put in additional time or require teacher's help, etc. Be as specific as possible)

Figure 1: Sample self-assessment form

Detailed corrections of notebooks and test papers

Maths problems were not just marked right or wrong; instead, clues were given on next steps, notes added on alternative methods and reasons provided on *why* a particular approach was considered 'incorrect' or 'incomplete'. The idea was to help students figure out what to do next and how to go about correcting their own errors.

In Figure 2, a student has drawn a pictogram to represent literacy rates in the four southern states of India. He has initially assigned an 'open book' symbol to a certain percentage value (note the scratched-out parts at the top) and then changed his mind to use a single circle to represent 100 per cent. The initial use of a more appropriate symbol indicates that the student understands not only what a pictogram is, but also how proportionality can be indicated through pictures.

The teacher's comments help point out that the student's initial approach is a better one. In this case, the comments prompted the student to reflect on why he discarded the first approach. It turned out that the decimal values threw him off. The teacher then asked him if rounding-off values resulted in loss of critical information. This helped the student figure out how to draw an appropriate pictogram.

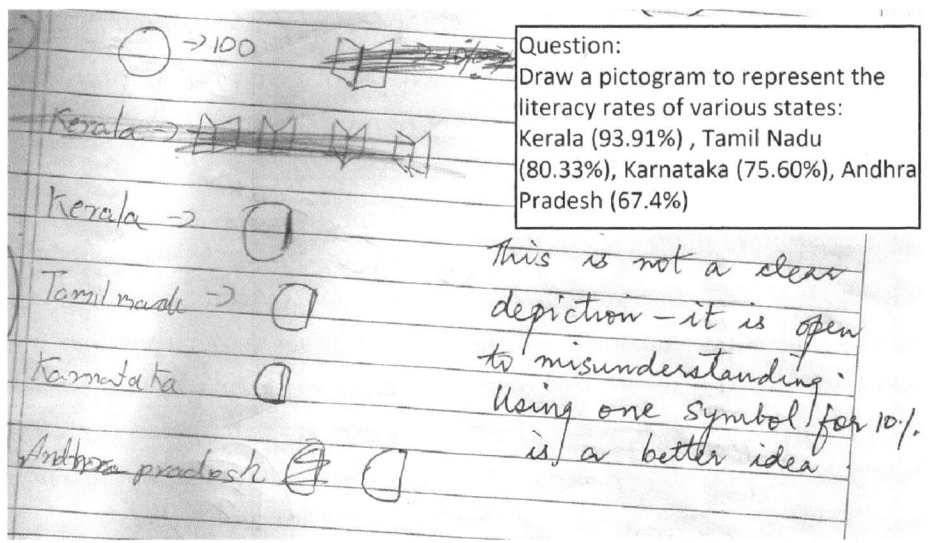

Figure 2: Correction with relevant tips

Instead of the teacher directly providing 'the one right answer' to the child, this approach encouraged the student to improve upon his previous work and come up with a better solution. Such corrections required more time and effort – requiring the teacher to look for what the child has understood and provide inputs on the next level of improvement. However, over time, it helped the teacher get a better sense of where each child was and helped her provide child-specific support. It also helped the child make step-by-step progress instead of feeling daunted by having too many mistakes to correct.

Push for participation in class

Each student had to participate and work out a problem in front of the entire class. The students were called in the order that they were seated. Knowing this order gave them the opportunity to start working on their problem in advance, so as to get ready for their turn. In case the student was not able to work out the problem, the student and teacher would together work it out on the board. The student would thus have to be alert and ready to work, but would, at the same time, get enough support not to feel humiliated or targeted. This helped many students gain confidence and also enabled learning from peers. It also enabled them to experience that making mistakes is not something to be worried or ashamed about – instead, it was something to learn from.

Answer keys with deliberate errors

After each test, as students' answer papers were collected for correction, they were, in turn, given an answer paper that *they* had to correct. The teacher deliberately introduced errors in this answer paper, based on the errors that she had noticed in their classwork and homework. The idea was to help students spot errors in the teacher's work – as it is often easier to spot errors in someone else's work. It was a special pleasure for some to comment on the teacher's mistakes. Figure 3 shows a sample answer sheet corrected by a student, with amusing comments to express his sentiments at the mistakes (note the fainting stick figure and 'Oh god' as reactions to some of the errors).

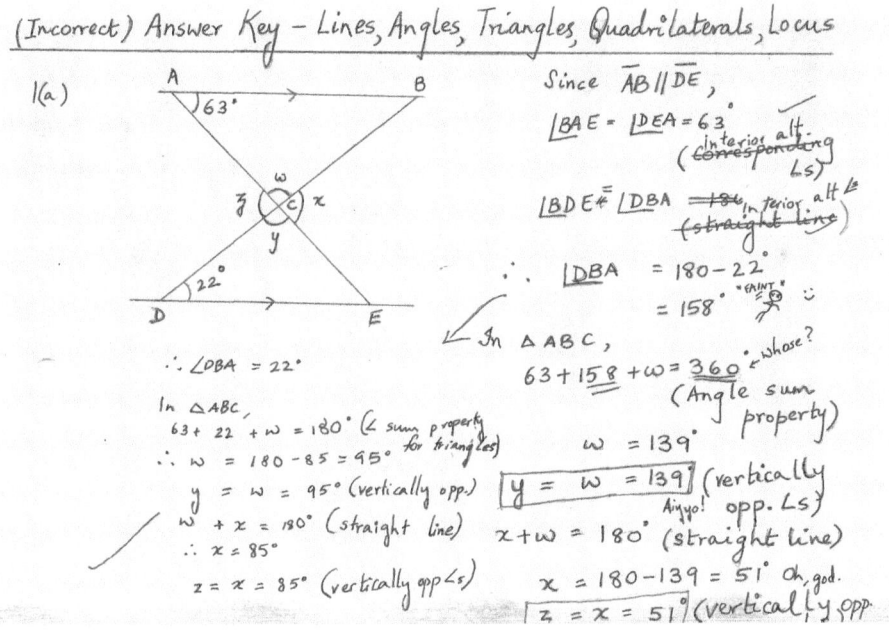

Figure 3: Correcting the teacher's answer

Answer keys with correct answers

After the corrected test scripts were returned to students, an answer key with the entire paper worked out, step by step, was given to each one. This gave them an opportunity to understand how to answer a given question as well as to correct their own work in detail.

Exam papers with additional scaffolding

Based on inputs from remedial teachers who worked with students requiring one-on-one support, exam papers were prepared with additional scaffolding to help students work towards an answer, step by step. Figure 4 shows an example of a question reframed to help students find the solution with step-by-step reasoning.

Question without scaffolding	Question with scaffolding
Find the distance between the points A and B shown in the graph below (graph is not shown to scale – do not measure using a ruler). 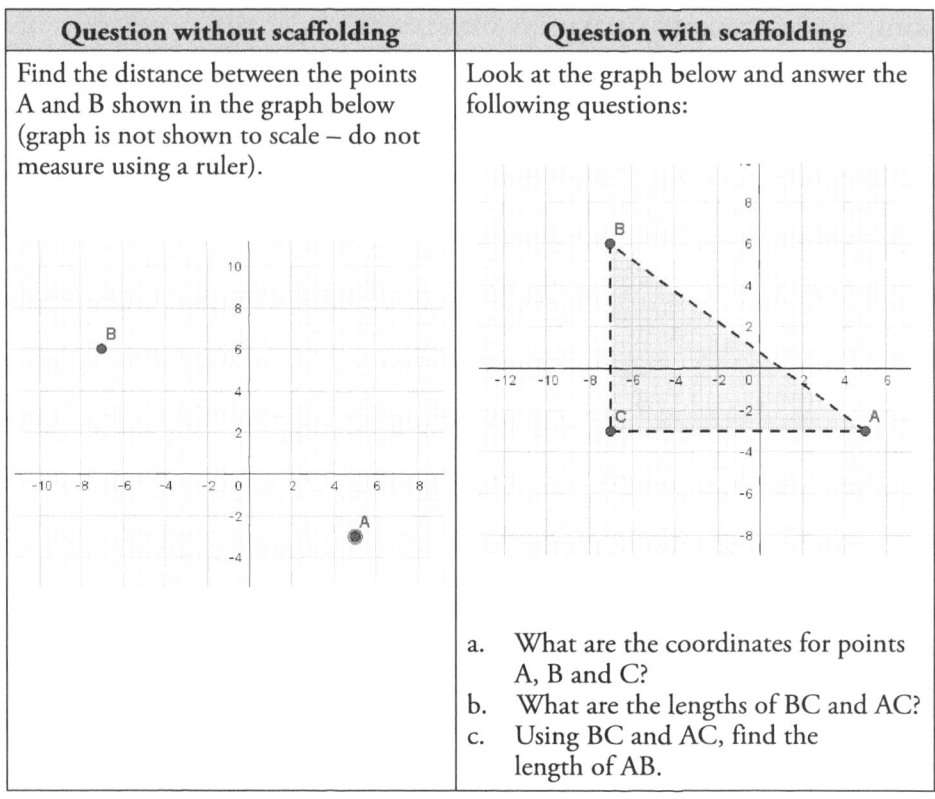	Look at the graph below and answer the following questions: a. What are the coordinates for points A, B and C? b. What are the lengths of BC and AC? c. Using BC and AC, find the length of AB.

Figure 4: Exam question with and without scaffolding

Categorising recurring errors

Gattegno (1954) challenges teachers to wonder at and question how certain kinds of errors are seen repeatedly, across maths classrooms around the world. Gleaning how a *student* understands a problem, or in Gattegno's words, analysing the *mental structures* that a student forms, while working with mathematical challenges, would help a teacher know how to teach better.

Errors encountered in a mathematics classroom probably outnumber correct solutions. Humour aside, the possible number of errors and their probable causes can be overwhelming to deal with. In this case, it helped to draw up categories of errors that could then be refined over time. These error categories helped simplify classroom communication and provided a framework that, in turn, identified appropriate strategies to tackle these categories. The error categories outlined, as follows, were drawn from classroom experiences and were grouped intuitively, by the teacher, to arrive at possible causes and eventually, likely solutions. These error categories are used throughout this paper to explain the process of error analysis followed in the classroom. The list of error categories, possible causes and strategies to counter them are by no means exhaustive and represent a 'work-in-progress', changing every year as new students and new experiences add to them.

Superficial errors

These errors are commonly referred to as 'careless mistakes', implying that the child knows enough *not* to commit them, but does so anyway. We prefer to call them 'superficial' errors as they do not usually reflect an issue with deeper understanding of the underlying mathematical principles or methods. Some examples of such errors are as follows:

1. *Recall errors* – These refer to mistakes in remembering specific formulae or steps in a multi-step problem.
2. *Copy errors* – These refer to mistakes in copying numbers or symbols from the question paper to the answer sheet, or in copying numbers from one step in the solution to the next. Figures 5 and 6 provide snapshots of two such errors. While the former is a minor error, the latter results in a significantly different answer due to the cascading effect of multiple steps.

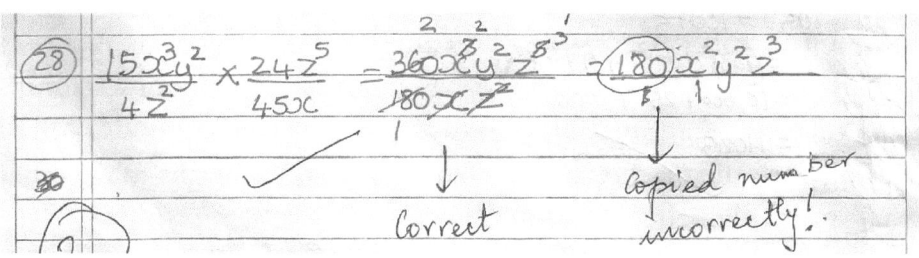

Figure 5: Copy error 1

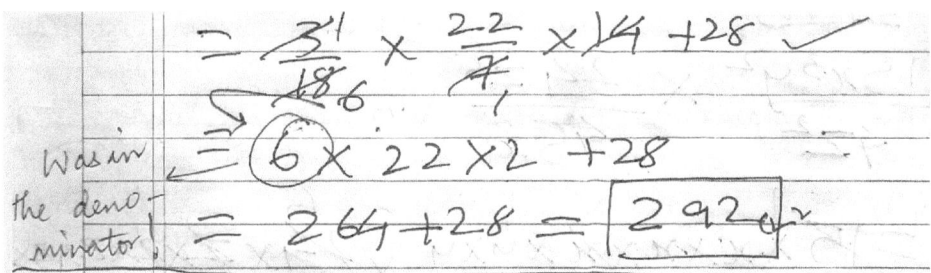

Figure 6: Copy error 2

Method-based errors

These errors typically occur when a student depends excessively or blindly on methods to solve a problem, instead of understanding the logic behind the steps. *Integer* and *fraction arithmetic errors* are common in this category. Figure 7 shows one such error.

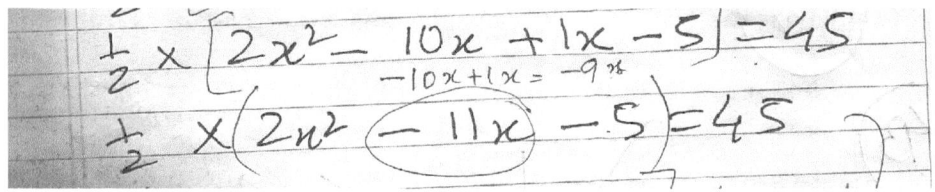

Figure 7: Error in integer arithmetic

Transposing errors while solving algebraic equations (e.g. $2x - \frac{y}{3} = 6 \Rightarrow 2x - y = 6 \times 3$), or *conjoining errors* while performing operations on algebraic expressions (e.g. $3xy + 6xy = 9x^2y^2$) are also common in this category. As the complexity of problems increases in high school, a purely method-based approach sometimes results in an incorrect combination of steps from different methods – often causing both the teacher and student to rack their brains to decipher what is actually being attempted!

Another unfortunate (though inevitable) fallout of these errors is that even when a student realises the meaning behind the method at a later point of time, some of the deep-seated method-related errors continue to persist for a while longer and are hard to unlearn. A sustained pattern of thinking takes time to be rooted out completely.

Comprehension errors

Comprehension errors include errors that arise from not being able to understand a new concept. The square-root operation is one such example – students typically substitute this operation with division (e.g. $\sqrt{36} = \frac{36}{2} = 18$)) until they are able to understand what the operation really means. Errors in visualising problems in geometry and understanding figures in mensuration also fall under this category.

Figure 8 shows an error committed by a student in establishing the congruency of two triangles. The two triangles *are* congruent, but the student has not been able to visualise how one triangle is identical to another when rotated.

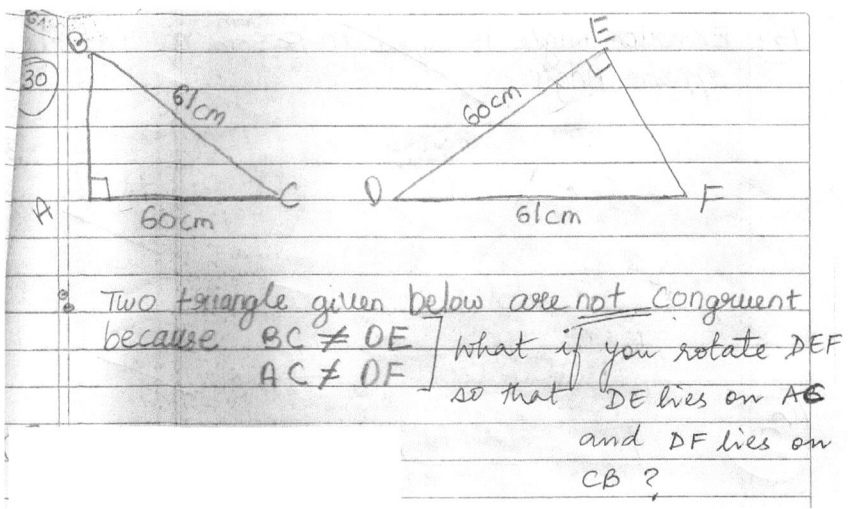

Figure 8: Comprehension error

Errors in using mathematical language

These errors arise from a difficulty in expressing one's thought process or logical deduction through appropriate mathematical language.

This can range from using inappropriate terms or properties to a seeming inability to theoretically prove a mathematical statement. While these may not strictly be 'errors', they nevertheless point out an important area that needs to be worked on, and hence are worth being categorised.

In Figure 9, the student is successfully proving that $\triangle ABC$ is similar to $\triangle EDC$. However, the language used is less formal. Use of appropriate symbols ($\overline{AB} \parallel \overline{DE}$ instead of $\overline{AB}$ is parallel to $\overline{DE}$), three-letter angle references ($\angle ACB = \angle ECD$ instead of $\angle C = \angle C$ and correct angle relationship names (Interior Alternate Angles instead of Z law) help express the proof in succinct and unambiguous mathematical language.

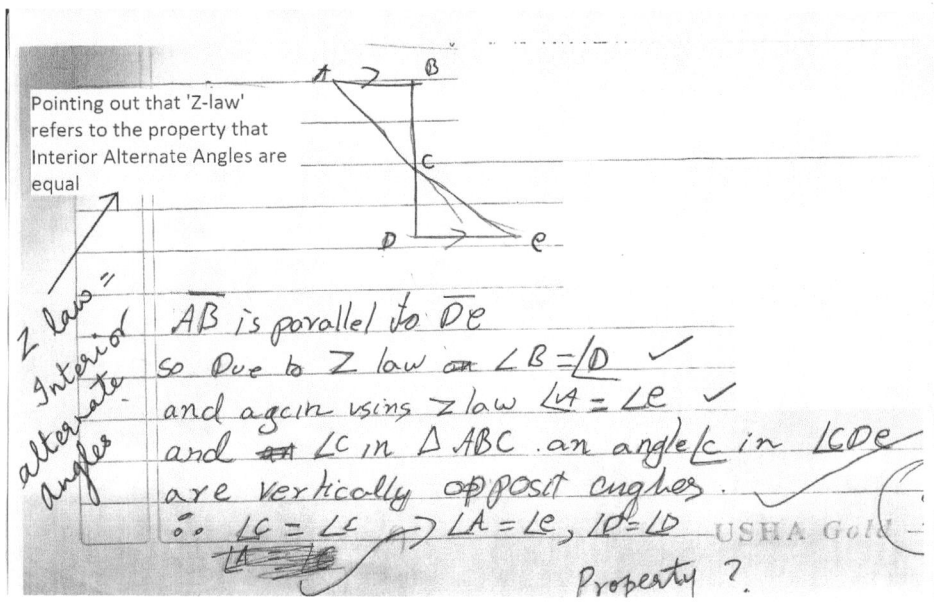

Figure 9: Incomplete use of mathematical language

Assigning errors to appropriate categories

Once terminology related to error categories was introduced to the students and discussed in class, the next step was to assign errors found in the students' work to appropriate categories. This section explains how the teacher and student analysed the cause of each specific error and then grouped the errors into appropriate categories.

The teacher's analysis of an error committed by a student was not always straightforward or simple. For example, Figure 10 shows how a student tried to compute the length of a square field, given its area.

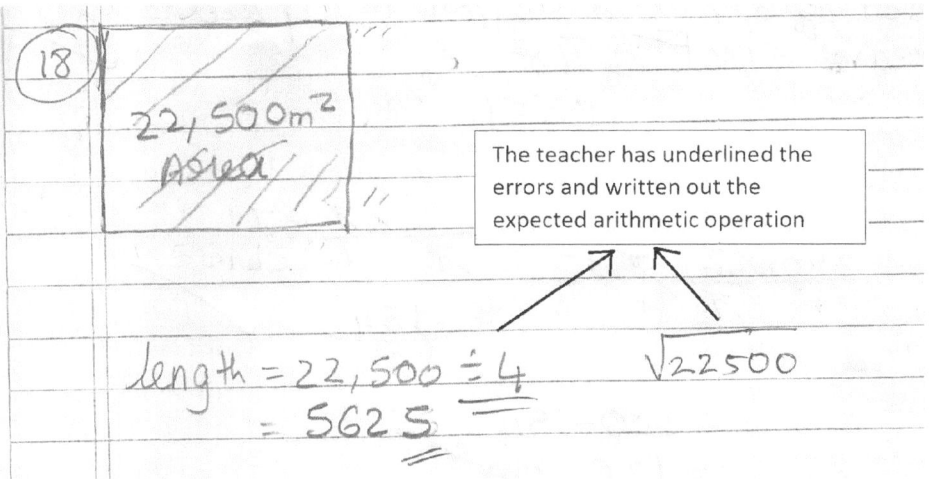

Figure 10: Error in calculating side of a square, given its area

The teacher analysed this error as follows:

✦ The student has correctly shaded the region inside the square – so there is probably no error in visualising the *area of the given shape.*

✦ The use of the formula $length = \frac{area}{4}$ by the student suggests one of the following: either it is a recall error, where the child has incorrectly used the perimeter formula instead of the area formula; or the child has not been able to grasp the square-root operation.

Since multiple possibilities existed, it was evident that the errors from one source alone (e.g. test correction) were not sufficient to understand the possible *cause* of error. Classroom interactions with the child, classwork and homework corrections and patterns of error in different tests, all helped narrow down the possible reasons for the error. In this case, it turned out to be a *comprehension error* as the child did not understand the square-root operation.

Once the teacher assigned errors to categories, it was the students' turn to analyse their mistakes and think about possible causes. Figure 11 shows a conversation between the teacher and student, where the teacher helped the student discover an error that he had committed. Once the student understood the error, the teacher (re)introduced appropriate terminology to help categorise it. In this conversation, based on an actual interaction, the error turned out to be a 'conjoin error', which was categorised as a method-based error.

Over a period of a few months, the teacher and student, together, identified and categorised errors in the student's work. For example, when the teacher called out an error as a recall error (e.g. incorrect formula used), the student came back and informed the teacher that it was not a superficial error, but a mistake committed due to a lack of understanding and hence a comprehension error.

Error analysis has not just been time-consuming but unrewarding, too, at times. It has not always been possible to generalise causes – a combination of errors complicated analysis further. What *has* always been useful, however, is to go through this process *with the students* so that they can take over and analyse their own errors after a point of time and figure out strategies that best help them. In our experience, most students of the class started analysing their errors and assigning them to appropriate categories by the end of a year of this process.

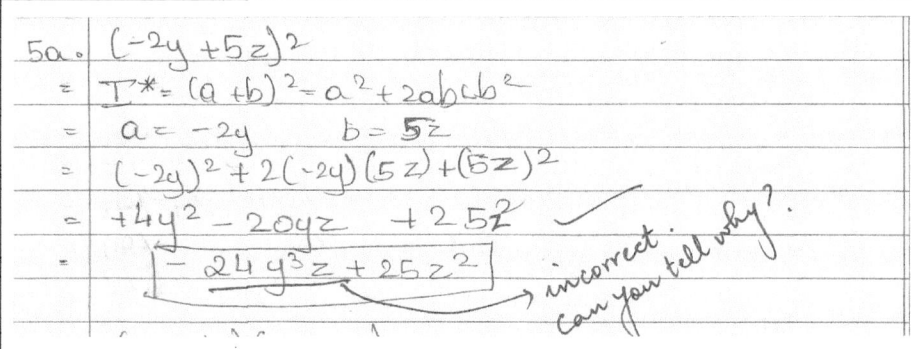

$$5a. \; (-2y + 5z)^2$$
$$= \; I* = (a+b)^2 = a^2 + 2ab + b^2$$
$$= \; a = -2y \qquad b = 5z$$
$$= \; (-2y)^2 + 2(-2y)(5z) + (5z)^2$$
$$= \; +4y^2 - 20yz + 25z^2 \quad \checkmark$$
$$= \; \boxed{-24y^3z + 25z^2}$$

incorrect. Can you tell why?

Teacher: Can you show me how you worked out the problem?

Student: (Works out the problem till he comes to the step where he has committed an error: $4y^2 - 20yz + 25z^2$)

Teacher: Are there any like terms?

Student: No.

Teacher: So, can I simplify the answer further?

Student: No. Oh … I understand – I have combined the first two terms by mistake!

Teacher: Right! Such an error is called a Conjoin Error.

Figure 11: Conversation on 'conjoin error' in algebra

Implementing strategies to reduce recurring errors

The possible causes for some common errors and strategies to overcome them keep evolving. In our experience, what worked for one student or a set of students sometimes needed to be tweaked or changed to help another. Though the sample set of errors are drawn from a specific group of students (described earlier in the section on sample group), the possible causes and strategies are drawn from the experience of all the mathematics and remedial teachers at Poorna

Learning Centre. It is also important to note that students contributed significantly and helped the teachers build this list over years.

This exercise involved the following three-step process:

1. The teacher and student assigned errors to specific categories.
2. They identified the top one or two error categories, student wise. For example, a student might look at his/her test paper and conclude that the majority of the errors were superficial errors, while the rest were comprehension errors.
3. This was followed by a discussion on how to target a specific error category and reduce the errors in this category.

The following sections highlight some possible causes for common errors and the strategies that were attempted to reduce these errors. The causes and strategies are explained against each error category (described earlier in the section on categorising recurring errors).

Superficial errors

A common cause for superficial errors was haste. Students were often in a hurry to complete their work, sometimes because of time constraint in a test, but also due to other reasons such as a compulsion to be the first to call out an answer, to be done with one's work as soon as possible or an excitement over figuring out what to do next. Helping students slow down, teaching them to revise their work, discouraging shouting out of answers and similar classroom practices that supported different paces of working were some strategies that helped a child work on superficial errors.

Another common cause for superficial errors, especially recall errors, was lack of practice. Encouraging students to work consistently throughout the year, instead of just before an evaluation, while also encouraging active participation in the classroom were some strategies that helped.

Two students drew our attention to one more cause for superficial errors. These two students had overcome superficial errors through consistent practice and a conscious revision of their work. When asked how the errors resurfaced in their exam paper, they explained that they were tense during the examination and this resulted in more errors. Stress related to examinations was probably a key cause for a large number of errors. Students, over time, came up with their own personalised strategies to combat this. For example, one child found that simple breathing exercises at the beginning of an exam helped. While there are no quick and easy solutions to handle exam-related stress, as teachers, we have found it useful to keep reminding students that despite these errors, we are aware that they *know* how to solve the problem. Hopefully, with time, this confidence-building exercise will lead to less performance anxiety during an examination.

Method-based errors

These errors have been the toughest to deal with. The first step was to determine whether the error arose from a lack of understanding or from an overdependence on the method. Sitting with students as they worked out a problem and asking appropriate questions, at each step, to gauge understanding was a strategy that helped narrow down the cause of error. If the students were able to spot the error on their own and correct it as the teacher asked a well-timed question, then it was not a comprehension issue. The conversation in Figure 12 illustrates this process. In this case, the student has understood the logic behind fraction addition but has blindly, and incorrectly, followed a method that has led her to a wrong answer.

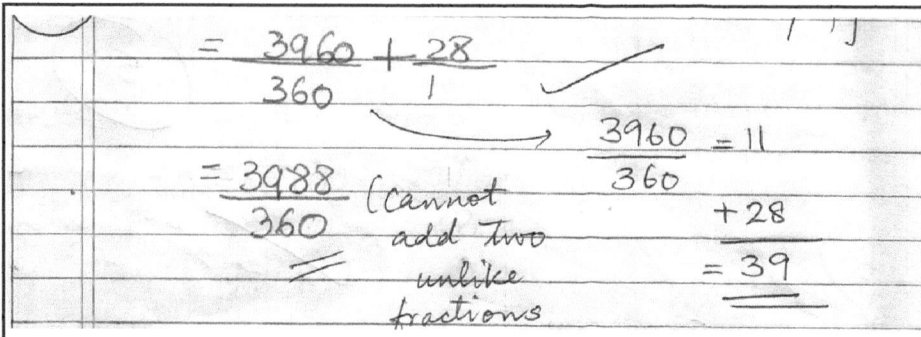

Teacher: Can you show me how you worked out the problem?

Student: (Works out the problem till she comes to the step where she has committed an error: 3960/360+ 28)

Teacher: What kind of numbers are these?

Student: One is a Fraction and the other is a Whole Number

Teacher: How do I add these?

Student: (Converts the Whole number to Fraction form: 3960/360+28/1)

Teacher: Ok, that brings them both to a Fraction form. Are they Like Fractions?

Student: (Thinks for a while and then says …) I got it, aunty, leave it.

Teacher: (Cue for the teacher to stop prodding. The student has understood that she has committed an error in adding two Unlike Fractions and is able to fix the error.)

Figure 12: Fraction arithmetic error

Conversations such as these not only helped check if an error was method-based but also enabled students to review their work, step by step, and spot these errors by themselves. Additionally, over a period of time, repeatedly pointing out the meaning behind the method (e.g. cancellation means dividing by the same factor) helped students pick up the associated vocabulary.

Comprehension errors

Errors in this category needed to be addressed on a case-by-case basis. Conversations with the students and notebook corrections helped understand if a child had an issue comprehending what was taught. An individual child's challenge in understanding a given topic helped drive the strategy required to catch and reduce errors in this category. Figure 13 shows a sample question on mensuration.

Q. Find the area of the shaded region in the figure below.

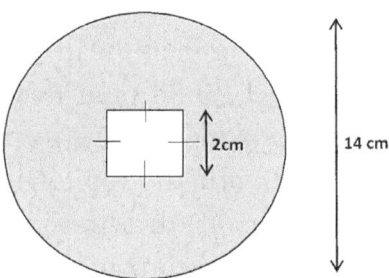

Figure 13: Question on mensuration

In class, the children were taught to break down the figure into constituent shapes – a circle and a square – and then to analyse and arrive at the area of the shaded figure (you get the shaded region once you remove the square piece from the circle). A remedial teacher, who provided after-school support to one of the students in the class, pointed out that this was not sufficient to help the child understand how to approach the problem. She had to work with him, step-by-step, before the child reached his 'aha' moment and was able to figure out what was expected. The following outline illustrates how she helped the child understand this problem:

✦ She realised that the child was not able to interpret the meaning of the double-headed arrow that indicated the diameter of the circle. She moved the arrow to align with a diameter inside the circle to help him understand the indicated measure.

✦ She then made the child cut out a circle on chart paper and then cut out a square from within the circle. He then matched the cut-out shape with the shape given in the problem.

✦ Once he crossed this crucial first step of being able to visualise how the shape was arrived at, it was easier for him to then use appropriate area formulae to calculate the area of the shaded region.

It was, of course, far easier to realise that students had not understood something, than to arrive at strategies to help them understand. The strategies included giving students more time with a question, helping them visualise using manipulatives or designing activities to help them draw a parallel (build their own mental structures). The errors in this category provided inputs to the teacher that a student may require more time with the topic. If multiple students' work showed comprehension errors, then this indicated to the teacher that an alternative teaching approach may be required for the topic.

Errors in using mathematical language

As explained earlier, this category did not always refer to an 'error', but more to an inability to express oneself mathematically. In class, it was common for children to use phrases like 'that thingy' or 'those angles', accompanied by a furious movement of hands and shoulders to mime out the relationship or property that they understood but were just not able to articulate. One reason for the delay in building their own mathematical language was their belief that they had met their goal as soon as they got the final answer. Sadly, it has been common in high-school mathematics to focus on arriving at the 'correct' answer, with not much regard for the process, logic or mathematical language used.

Highlighting that mathematics had its own language and that it was important to use appropriate words in the appropriate context was a process that had to be integrated into the regular classroom through the academic year. Insisting that students use the right mathematical terms, while simultaneously acknowledging what they already knew, is a strategy that has yielded results in our classrooms over years. It has been important to strike a balance between pushing but not frustrating students. Figure 14 shows an example of appropriate use of mathematical language (the problem was to find the value of missing angles in a figure with two parallel lines and a triangle).

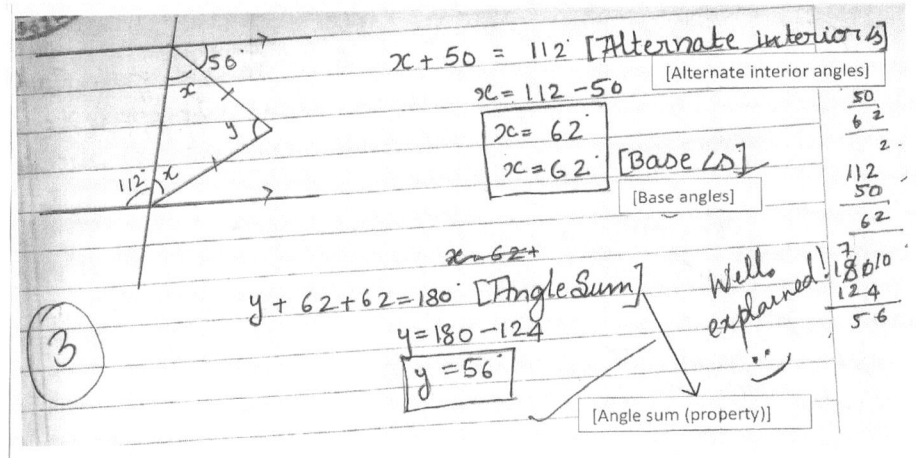

Figure 14: Using appropriate mathematical language

An important point that the teacher realised early on was that mathematical *thinking* should be encouraged irrespective of whether or not the child was able to express a solution in mathematical language. Encouraging alternative solutions, as well as ways of expressing them, and allowing a student to challenge the conventional mode of answering were an important part of stimulating logical and deductive reasoning. Figure 15 shows a student's answer as an example of an alternative approach to a problem and a different style of responding – he enjoyed answering in a narrative style.

Question: The student had to decide which option was better – buying two pizzas of diameter 12 cm each or buying one pizza of diameter 24 cm.

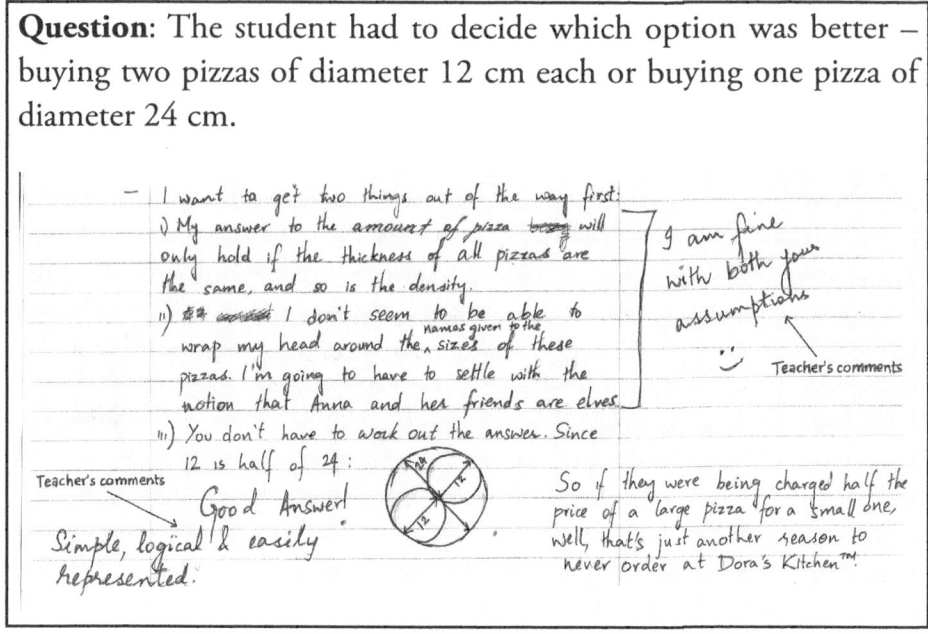

Figure 15: Alternative approach to answering

Table 1 summarises the common errors, their possible causes and proposed strategies to counter them, which have been discussed in this paper.

Table 1: Summary of errors, causes and strategies

Error category	Possible causes	Proposed strategies
Superficial errors (often referred to as 'careless mistakes'; e.g. copy and recall errors)	Haste	Encourage students to slow down, be sensitive to different working speeds and revise their work.
	Lack of practice	Encourage students to work consistently through the year and actively participate in the classroom.
	Examination stress	Conduct confidence-building exercises; encourage students to come up with their own personalised stress-management strategies.

Error category	Possible causes	Proposed strategies
Method-based errors (e.g. skipping a step, mixing up steps and combining steps from two different operations)	Blindly following a method-based approach in problem-solving	Prompt students with leading questions as they work out the problem step by step; repeatedly explain/review the meaning behind specific methods (e.g. cancellation and converting fractions to like fractions).
Comprehension errors (e.g. not being able to understand the square-root operation and visualisation challenges in mensuration)	Need for alternate ways of understanding and tackling the problem (e.g. visual learners versus kinaesthetic learners)	Use student-specific strategy: work one-on-one with the child, providing extra time, using manipulatives and activities, etc.
Errors in using mathematical language (e.g. using inappropriate or incorrect mathematical terms and inability to justify a deduction)	Stress only on finding the final answer, but not enough on the deductive process; insufficient use of, or exposure to, mathematical language	Insist on using mathematically appropriate terms and diagrams, while still encouraging mathematical thinking (e.g. alternative styles of expression); stress on mathematics having its own language of expression through examples and constant usage.

Observations and Learning

This section provides information both from the teacher's and student's perspectives. Data for this section was collected through review of student notebooks, tests and examinations; classroom interactions; self-evaluation forms (written by students); Parent Teacher Meeting (PTM) reports (written by the teacher); and one-on-one interviews with the students.

Teacher observations and learning

Error analysis has helped us teachers don a learner's hat. The process has helped add several strategies to spot and tackle errors of different kinds to the bag of 'teacher's tools'. Additionally, the process has also helped change some of the teachers' preconceptions on how children learn and reflect. There have been two important learnings for the teacher, which are discussed as follows:

1. *The first key learning has been that the effort spent on creating an environment where mistakes can be openly discussed and debated is effort well spent.* Martin et al. (2005) describe one such classroom where the mathematics teacher helps his students develop appropriate mathematical language and mathematical reasoning by supporting them through an inquiry-based approach. The research by Schleppenbach et al. (2007) talks about the importance of creating an environment where students feel free to make mistakes, analyse and discuss them, in order to learn from them. This is in contrast with classroom practices that cast a negative light on errors, with teachers prohibiting, hiding or ignoring errors. The latter creates a fear of mistakes in students, making them believe that mistakes make them look 'bad' and should thus not be discussed.

   As described earlier (see the section on creating an environment for error analysis), before jumping into the identification of errors, their possible causes and strategies to tackle them, it was important to get students comfortable with the idea of discussing errors without the additional baggage of embarrassment or shame. This meant slowing down and deliberating on processes that put children at ease and seeking feedback from them – either directly or through classroom observation. While this was particularly challenging in secondary classes (Grades IX and X) with Board Exam pressure omnipresent, spending time to create the right environment at the beginning helped save time towards the end; students started independently working on strategies that helped them rather than expecting teachers to direct them – thus speeding up the process of self-learning and correction.

Table 2 describes the effectiveness of some of the strategies applied to help create an appropriate environment for error analysis. Success of a strategy was gauged as follows:

✦ Successful: More than 50 per cent of the class benefitted from the strategy (e.g. positive response to repeatedly using the strategy, greater classroom participation, more clarity in expressing thoughts, increased confidence in defending one's ideas and better performance in tests).

✦ Moderately successful: About 25 to 50 per cent of the students benefitted from the strategy.

✦ Unsuccessful: No student or hardly any students benefitted from the strategy.

Of course, the same set of strategies did not always work for a new batch of children. It is worthwhile to continuously add to the list of strategies, and also retain those that did not work – as they may work for a different group of children or with minor modifications.

Table 2: Effectiveness of strategies used to create an environment for analysis

Strategy used	Effectiveness of strategy	Comments
Self-assessment after every topic	◯	This helped children understand how to break up topics and gauge their own understanding. However, none of them continued with this approach once the teacher asked them to create their own self-assessment forms. Probably too effort-consuming.

Contd...

Strategy used	Effectiveness of strategy	Comments
Detailed corrections of notebooks and test papers	☆	Even children who did not make the suggested corrections benefitted from knowing what to do next and understanding the kind of errors they tended to make.
Push for participation in class	☆	Though initially a cause for student anxiety, over a period of time, students started preparing for their turn and became comfortable working out problems in front of the whole class.
Answer keys with deliberate errors	⊘	Except for a very small percentage of the class, students did not turn in their corrections of these answer scripts. Worse still, some assumed they were the correct answers and used them as a reference for future problems!
Answer keys with correct answers	☆	Students preferred getting an answer key to compare their test scripts with, instead of copying down the correct answer from the blackboard. The usefulness of this strategy and the lack of success in the previous strategy probably indicates that the children were more interested in figuring out how to correct the errors that *they* had committed.
Tips on how to analyse errors	◯	This is still a work-in-progress strategy. Children seem to find it useful to have specific category names for the errors that they make. It helps them narrow down on one or two error categories that they need to focus on.

Strategy used	Effectiveness of strategy	Comments
Exam papers with additional scaffolding	◯	This strategy is a temporary strategy as students need to be slowly weaned away from requiring this scaffolding. It has been moderately useful in helping children understand how to break-up a problem and tackle it step by step.

Legend: Successful Moderately successful Unsuccessful

☆   ◯   🚫

2. *The second important takeaway has been the realisation that different children take different paths and different lengths of time to reach their 'zone of comfort' with mathematics.* While this learning may seem like an obvious conclusion, teachers needed to practically experience this in order to come to terms with what the process of teaching-learning entailed.

To flesh out one aspect of this learning: we have often found ourselves complaining about superficial, or method-based understanding, versus a deeper, application-based understanding of the subject. Though some students 'got' the problem, we would lament the fact that they did so only superficially. However, as we viewed the progress of children over a longer time frame (three to five years), we realised that different children made the journey towards deeper understanding in their own ways. While some started off with pure pattern-matching and method-based solutions, they added layers to their learning as their foundation grew stronger. They were able to make the transition to deeper and more intuitive understanding, with practice. The key ingredient in each such case was *consistent practice*.

Figure 16 captures our observation on increasing comfort level with mathematics of the children in our sample over a period of three years (with the 2015 values being the baseline for comparison). Here, 'comfort level' indicates a deeper understanding of the topics and not just mastering exam-writing skills. It has been measured through the following parameters: test/exam performance, clarity in reasoning in the classroom, ability to justify one's solution, ability to make cross-topic connections and ability to teach another student.

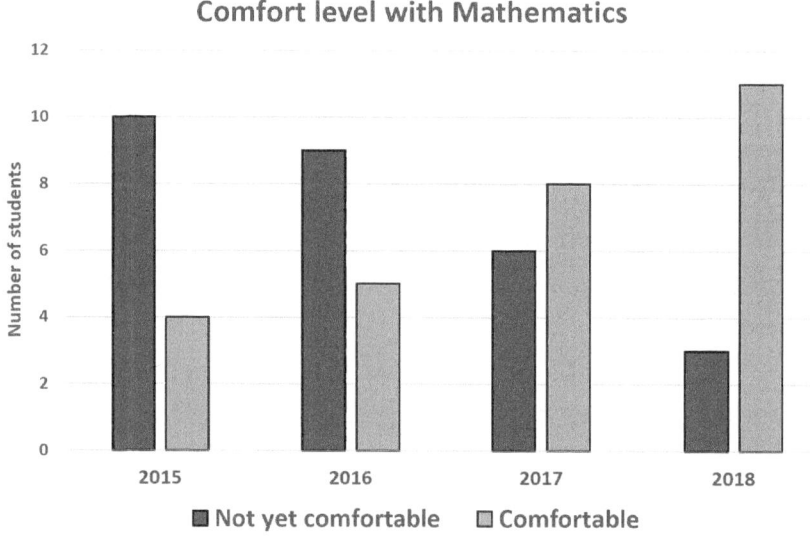

Figure 16: Multi-year progress of students in mathematics

Student observations and learning

All the 14 students in the sample set were interviewed face-to-face by the author and asked to reflect on the processes followed in class (see the section on creating an environment for error analysis) and various strategies suggested (see the section on implementing strategies to reduce recurring errors) in the last few years. They were requested to provide feedback on strategies that they experienced as being useful and those that they did not. They were also encouraged to share successful strategies that they had themselves tried out. The interview was informal and allowed the students an opportunity to dwell on observations that *they* believed were significant.

Table 3 lists what the students thought about the effectiveness of various strategies. Success of a strategy was determined as follows:

✦ Successful: 50 per cent or more of the students believed that the strategy had helped them in one way or the other (e.g. reduced the occurrence of a specific type of error, increased their confidence in class and helped them communicate their mathematical ideas better).

✦ Moderately successful: About 25 to 50 per cent of the students believed that the strategy had helped them.

✦ Unsuccessful: Hardly any student believed that the strategy had helped him/her.

Table 3: Effectiveness of strategies and processes used in the maths classroom

Strategy suggested/ process followed in class	Error categories addressed	Effectiveness of strategy	Comments
Strategy: Slow down, be sensitive to different working speeds of classmates, revise your work	Superficial errors	◯	This strategy helped reduce superficial errors in classwork as well as in tests. However, peer pressure, to complete one's work as soon as possible, continued to be a significant driving force in tests and examinations.

Contd...

Strategy suggested/ process followed in class	Error categories addressed	Effectiveness of strategy	Comments
Strategy: Work consistently through the year and actively participate in the classroom	All: Superficial errors, method-based errors, comprehension errors, errors in using mathematical language	★	There was a reduction in all error categories when students followed this strategy – over the course of an academic year and year on year.
Strategy: Confidence-building exercises, student-specific stress-management strategies	Superficial errors, method-based errors, errors in using mathematical language	◯	While confidence-building strategies helped with classroom performance, students needed more time to handle exam-related stress.
Strategy: Use Answer Key with correct answers to spot your errors and work on correcting them	All	☆	All children found the answer key, with step-by-step worked out answers useful in reviewing their own answers.
Strategy: Classifying errors and identifying the type of errors that they committed most	All	☆	All students found that classification helped them analyse their errors and identify the top categories that they needed to work on.

Strategy suggested/ process followed in class	Error categories addressed	Effectiveness of strategy	Comments
Process: Creating an environment to discuss errors openly in class	All	☆	All students said that the processes followed in the class helped them discuss errors without experiencing fear or embarrassment. They found it useful to discuss their own and others' mistakes – it helped them learn better.
Process: Asking each student to work out a problem in front of the class, in rotation.	All	☆	Students confessed that they initially felt anxious or embarrassed working out a problem in front of the whole class. However, watching their classmates do it and getting support from the teacher helped them become more confident over time. Watching others solve problems also helped them understand how different people approach and think through a problem.

Legend: Successful   Moderately successful   Unsuccessful

The following are two significant findings that emerged from this interview process with the students:

1. *Firstly, each student had reached the same conclusion that practice helped them improve their mathematical skills and this led to an increased interest in the subject.* Even those who did not practise on a regular basis, but did so sporadically, believed that they understood better and performed better in class and in tests, when they practised.

2. *Secondly, the students were able to analyse their own progress* over the last few years and talk about their current challenges and their strategies to overcome them. Statements like 'I used to make more *copy errors* before, but I now make time for revision and these errors have reduced' were made by most of the students interviewed. All students had a clear opinion on where they were three years ago, what worked for them and what they planned to work on next.

These findings were compared with the teacher's observations in class and overall test performance of each of the 14 children. Table 4 summarises the overlap in the teacher's and students' observations: where both believed that progress had been made.

Table 4: Overlap in teacher's and students' observations

Commonly observed progress	Number of students
Benefitted from an environment that helped discuss errors openly. Did not experience shame or fear in the classroom.	14
Had developed the ability to analyse one's own progress over the last three years and articulate it with specific examples.	11
Had developed the ability to use specific error categories to narrow down common causes of errors in their own work.	10
Were able to reduce the number of errors in their work through the process of error analysis, followed by practice.	10
Had developed the ability to directly correlate effort put in to improved understanding and performance in class.	14

Reflections

Error analysis started off initially as our effort to identify common errors committed by students in the mathematics class. The plan was to narrow down possible reasons for these errors, with the intention of helping students implement appropriate strategies to overcome them.

What evolved over a period of time was a change in attitude and approach to errors, both for the teacher and students involved. As the famous Chinese proverb goes, 'Give a man a fish and you feed him for a day. Teach a man to fish and you feed him for a lifetime.' Instead of just pointing out errors to the students, helping them analyse their own errors has been a very fruitful experience for us. While it has been useful to broadly categorise errors and work on common strategies to overcome them, the end goal was not only to come up with an exhaustive list of errors and strategies. During the process of interviewing children, what emerged as most satisfying was that they have started analysing their own errors and hence their own progress. The teacher continues to play an important role in pointing out patterns and nudging the student to reflect, but the student has now started donning the more crucial role of a self-learner.

Observations such as 'I was embarrassed and scared in class two years back because I was the only one who did not know maths; but now I can work out problems on my own' and 'I now actually have fun doing maths. When I don't feel like studying, I put on music and do maths problems' are statements that effortlessly summarise arduous journeys made by students who are no less than heroes who have scaled mountains.

The journey of self-analysis and reflection is a never-ending one. While continuing to work on this as teachers, encouraging new batches of children to reflect and self-learn, another idea that we hope to implement in the future is to encourage children to frame their own problem statements for Action Research projects. We also hope to facilitate short-term Student Action Research projects (e.g. how to reduce errors due to incorrect copying of numbers from the question paper) and help students monitor their own progress.

Conclusion

The process of error analysis has resulted in a mindset change in our classroom. True to Dweck's (2006) idea of a 'Growth Mindset', these children now believe that their mathematical abilities are not fixed, but something that can be honed and improved upon with practice.

While some strategies proved to be more successful than others, what has evolved is a joint teacher-student venture where each helps the other identify common errors and adds to the common toolkit of strategies to overcome such errors. This process has helped create a certain classroom culture where errors are not feared but analysed and discussed openly.

Error analysis is a long-term process. It requires continuous revision and addition – a process that helps both the teacher and student evolve. For us, investing in this effort has proved worthwhile.

References

Bouvier, A. 1987. 'The Right to Make Mistakes'. *For the Learning of Mathematics* 7: 17-25.

Dweck, C. S. 2006. *Mindset: The New Psychology of Success.* New York: Ballantine Books.

Gattegno, C. 1954. 'Mathematics and the Child. III: The Use of Mistakes in the Teaching of Mathematics'. *The Mathematical Gazette* 38(323): 11-14.

Lockhart, P. 2009. *A Mathematician's Lament.* New York: Bellevue Literary Press.

Martin, T. S., S. M. McCrone, M. L. Bower and J. Dindyal. 2005. 'The Interplay of Teacher and Student Actions in the Teaching and Learning of Geometric Proof'. *Educational Studies in Mathematics* 60(1): 95-124.

Schleppenbach, M., L. M. Flevares, L. M. Sims and M. Perry. 2007. 'Teachers' Responses to Student Mistakes in Chinese and U.S. Mathematics Classrooms'. *The Elementary School Journal 108*(2): 131-147.

Swartz, R. 1976. 'Mistakes as an Important Part of the Learning Process'. *The High School Journal 59*(6): 246-257.

Disclaimer: The questions that have been provided as a sample, to exemplify typical errors associated with a student's answer, have been taken from multiple sources – mathematics textbooks for high school, past question papers from different examination boards (including Cambridge IGCSE and NIOS Boards, in particular) as well as worksheets and question papers created by teachers, both within Poorna Learning Centre and outside. I do not claim them to be original, nor do I claim ownership over any of them. Their use in this paper is to highlight the errors in a student's answer rather than to draw attention to a question itself.

Acknowledgements

I would like to thank Dr Neeraja Raghavan, Founder-Director, Thinking Teacher, for introducing me to the idea of error analysis, providing several valuable inputs on how to implement it in the classroom and also encouraging me to write this paper.

I would also like to thank Ms Jayanthi Sachitanand, Director-Trustee, Poorna Learning Centre, for her inexhaustible drive to implement a supportive learning environment at Poorna. She has played a key role in initiating the idea of this paper and providing valuable inputs from her own experience. I am deeply grateful to Ms Hemalatha Gowda, Physics and Mathematics Teacher, Poorna Learning Centre, for her untiring support and readiness to apply new strategies in the classroom. This paper would not have been possible without her constant inputs and numerous detailed discussions on her classroom experiences. I would also like to thank Ms Saira Banu, Principal, Poorna Learning Centre, and Dr Indira Vijaysimha, Founder-Trustee, Poorna Learning Centre, for their constant encouragement and support to help me develop and grow as a teacher and a person.

Experience is simply the name we give our mistakes.

Oscar Wilde

DRAWING OUT THE REFLECTIVE LEARNER

Overview

In the preceding chapters, the four teacher-researchers attempted to illustrate to their students (and, in turn, to the readers) how mistakes reveal many 'missed takes'. While each one developed his/her own route towards the same goal, there were several common findings.

Teachers found that the thought process of the erring student revealed itself more and more, as the research progressed. The students, in turn, slowed down and became less obsessed with swiftly arriving at the 'right answer', and in so doing, they reaped rich benefits. If one student experienced the change wrought by the simple act of according due attention to carefully reading the questions (and thus, correctly copying the information therein), another discovered the impact of the equally simple practice of going over the answered worksheet once, before turning it in. In the (carefully created) non-threatening atmosphere, several students realised that they were multiplying instead of adding, or that a very basic concept which they had assumed they had grasped (like place value) actually needed revisiting. Some of them learnt that just by having the text read aloud with varying intonations, they could carry out punctuation correctly – a task that they had found very difficult until then. A few needed to sit with the teacher initially to figure out why a certain answer was 'wrong', while some needed very little nudging before they declared that they had 'got it'.

As students began to feel empowered by the process of looking freely at their own mistakes, they experienced a release from being judged or overwhelmed with despair. Further, as they waded through the task of systematically examining and addressing their errors, their interest in the subject gradually picked up. Undoubtedly, their most surprising takeaway was the discovery that the same subject which had intimidated or bored them earlier now stimulated and challenged them. The initial investment of extra time and effort by each teacher resulted in the (inevitable) enhancement of enjoyment in learning for several students who participated in the research.

In this concluding chapter, an attempt is made to tie together the varied approaches that were adopted by the four teachers, by connecting them to broad underpinnings in research literature. Questions such as whether such research can be conducted across subjects, or is restricted to English and maths (the two subjects explored in this book), are raised and elaborated upon. Typical concerns in the minds of potential teacher-researchers are then addressed. For ease of reference, the routes followed by the four teacher-researchers are depicted in flow charts here, so as to afford a bird's eye view of the varied processes employed by them. This is presented with the intent of enabling the reader to select – from the methods used here – those elements that may suit their own context. Finally, a few suggestions are offered to the interested teacher or parent who may wish to try out such an approach in the classroom or at home. A broad roadmap is pictorially represented for interested readers to devise their own strategies to carry out such research.

The next section looks at the findings of these teacher-researchers, in order to examine the connections, if any, to what research has to say on the subject of awakening the reflective learner.

Through the Lens of Research Literature

None of these teacher-researchers began their work by doing a literature survey. As described in the preceding chapters, their work evolved organically after they first identified their concerns, and then proceeded to meet the demands of their unique situations. It was only during the documentation phase that one of them (Kanchana Suryakumar) read a few relevant research papers and began to see certain connections.

Without any intent to present a comprehensive review of the research in this domain, a few research papers in the area of studying mistakes are discussed below.

When did errors begin to be examined? And how?

How long have errors been the focus of research in the world of education research? According to Schleppenbach et al. (2007), only in the early nineties did the research on student errors in mathematics shift its approach by treating errors as resources for promoting learning. Until then, errors were mostly regarded as undesirable or merely as diagnostic tools. Ball (1991) advocated that teachers need to move beyond 'right' and 'wrong', and instead, use mistakes as a window to a student's thinking. This evolved into Cognitively Guided Instruction (CGI), which is nothing but basing one's instruction on the way that students think – and therefore, *first figuring out how students think* (Fennema et al. 1993; 1996). The reader has encountered illustrative examples for this in this compilation: Kanchana provided questions with and without scaffolding, for example, when she sensed the need to differentiate the way in which questions were posed, due to the different needs of students. Gopi showcased this approach by continuously adapting his method of instruction to suit the way that his students were thinking. This is also evident in the way that Prerna as well as Michael adapted their respective pedagogies to address the errors made by their students – while Prerna evolved strategies to help her fifth graders master spelling and punctuation, Michael pitched higher with his eighth graders by nudging them to think about their errors.

The following paragraphs give the gist of two papers – 'When Children Make Mistakes in Spelling' (Swearingen 1952) and 'The Use of Mistakes in the Teaching of Mathematics' (Gattegno 1954) – in order to provide a flavour of the typical concerns in English and mathematics, respectively. (The choice of subjects is purely based on the work that is described in this book.)

In his paper 'When Children Make Mistakes in Spelling', Swearingen (1952) reported an interesting evaluative study of a school programme which was triggered by the faculty's concern over students' persisting difficulty in the area of spelling in English. Curious to understand the situations when students tended to make more spelling errors, the faculty examined the spelling errors of third, fourth, fifth and sixth graders under four different conditions as part of their action research: during standardised achievement tests, in spelling lists containing commonly recognised spelling demons, informal tests of spellings of words from the textbooks and finally, in samples of the students' writing – from their stories, compositions and letters. They found that omissions (like apostrophes, capitals and silent letters) accounted for the largest percentage of errors, while substitutions (usually phonetic like *rane* for *rain*) came second. Many of the substitutions, in fact, were intelligent applications of phonetic knowledge. Among their very interesting conclusions were the following:

✦ When children write purposefully (e.g. letters, stories or compositions) they are likely to make fewer spelling errors than when attending to spelling lists. Thus, the spelling of a word in context is far more significant to the learner than a word taken out of context.

✦ Most children *want to* spell correctly when they write purposefully.

✦ There are not many children who write words without some thought about phonetics or meaning.

The reader can easily glean from the above conclusions that spelling errors are contextual, and that when the learner experiences some meaning in whatever is being written, there is far more effort to spell words rightly. This is corroborated by the finding of all the teacher-researchers here that there is often a thought process or logic behind each error.

Further, Swearingen (1952) stated that the faculty also analysed the errors with groups of children, as well as individually, in order to develop in the students a sense of responsibility for their self-improvement. They even went so far as to share the information with parents so as to garner their support in developing the spelling skills of their children.

On the role of context in enhancing writing skill, the research conducted by the teachers discussed in this volume present similar narratives. For instance, Michael's brief engagement with Lakshman brought home to the student the context, and therefore, nudged him into replacing his first choice of verb (*driving* a plane) with the right one (*flying* a plane). Prerna, too, drew out her students' sense of responsibility in conquering spelling errors by having each student draw up a spelling list that was unique to his/her need, which proved to be far more meaningful than a common spelling list for the entire class.

In his succinct paper titled 'The Use of Mistakes in the Teaching of Mathematics', Gattegno (1954) examined how mistakes made by students in mathematics can be turned to the teacher's advantage. As per his first piece of advice, a teacher should curb the tendency to correct, and instead *make use of the mistakes that have been committed by students* by incorporating these into the daily lesson. His categorisation of typical mistakes in algebra and geometry would ring familiar to the reader of Kanchana's and Gopi's research, which raised the question (that he, too, asked): why are mistakes in mathematics so universal and so similar?

By way of answering this question, Gattegno went so far as to declare: 'Mistakes are mainly due to mishandling of mental situations on the part of the teacher.' Moreover, he made a very profound assertion: *similar mistakes imply similar mental structures*, and as long as these mental structures are left unexamined by the teacher, the same set of mistakes will be encountered year after year by the teacher, with different batches of students. On the other hand, teachers who use mistakes as guiding lights into the students' minds will empower students to gain mental structures that are akin to mathematical structures. Gopi began his research with exactly the same intent – of entering the students' minds – and was rewarded with the explicit feedback when his student declared that mathematics was no longer mere computation for him, but that it now represented a way of thinking.

Can Mistakes Turn into 'Missed Takes' only in English and Mathematics?

Given the selection of case studies represented in this book, this is an inevitable question that will arise in the reader's mind. As stated at the outset, the choice of subjects was not that of the facilitator of this research (also the compiler of this book). It so happened that teachers who expressed interest in joining the Reflective Learner Programme were either English or mathematics teachers.

However, such a scrutiny is equally feasible in other subjects as well. Every subject demands the mastery of certain content and development of a particular set of skills. If the teacher can first spend some time articulating these, then this will not only set the stage for examining error patterns, it will also give the teacher a robust understanding of the learning outcomes of that particular content. Table 1 represents a general checklist to guide the potential teacher-researcher. It can be adapted to any specific subject and grade concerned.

Table 1: Checklist of content and skills

Content knowledge	Skills
Recall of factual knowledge, e.g. dates and names of battles.	Clear and articulate expression of knowledge, skill of clear and articulate enquiry.
Understanding of a concept, e.g. understanding why things float or sink.	Ability to apply the understanding – making a boat that floats with the appropriate materials.
General knowledge of related information (not necessarily taught in class), e.g. knowledge of the names of important cities in Europe is necessary before locating their neighbouring cities on a map.	Ability to represent the understanding – through a map, graph, diagram, etc.
Pre-requisite knowledge for the concerned grade e.g. knowledge of symbols and valencies is needed before learning how to write chemical formulae.	Experimental skills, computational skills, vocabulary.
Interconnectedness of newly learnt content to prior knowledge, e.g. seeing how the laws of motion are at play in a game of carom.	Problem-solving, hypothesising, verifying hypotheses.

Just as students are lost when it comes to error analysis until they understand what constitutes an error, teachers need this kind of clarity before embarking on research that strives to understand why students commit errors. It is therefore advisable for the teacher-researcher to begin research by first compiling a table like Table 1. Having carried out the above exercise, the teacher can then take the first step on the journey of error analysis.

How Can an Interested Teacher Carry out Such Research?

The very first challenge for a teacher who undertakes to systematically examine mistakes is the mindset of students as well as adults (be they parents or teachers). Students who have not previously been expected to self-regulate their study are unlikely to meet such a demand with ease. As Pierce and Kalkman (2003) point out, many students may even feel threatened when they are expected to don such a role. Not surprisingly, therefore, Gopi experienced intense resistance from his students when he demanded that they slow down and show him the four stages in solving a problem. Prerna discovered that she had to invest an unexpectedly long period (an entire month out of her four-month-long research) in addressing student fears and resistance to such an exercise. Michael, too, experienced resistance initially from the students, when he asked them to analyse their error patterns. When he switched to getting them to identify where they had written *correctly*, this task appealed to them far more. He then transitioned his approach to error analysis slowly, after the students' minds were readied for such a scrutiny. Kanchana pushed her students first to participate in class, until they saw that mistakes were nothing to be ashamed of.

What are the other ways of creating this kind of ambience?

Schleppenbach et al. (2007) assert that asking students questions about their errors is a very effective way of creating a climate for inquiry. They also emphasise that these questions should be varied, and not just revolve around finding out why a mistake has been made. Such an approach results in students seeing multiple ways of solving a mathematical problem, for example, and indeed, this was the experience of Gopi's students.

During such exploratory sessions, it is inevitable that the following question will be raised: Why are mistakes made at all? Bouvier (1987) asserts something that these teacher-researchers discovered, i.e. 'Mistakes are not the result of chance. They show that the student has used a particular logic, although not the appropriate one.' For example, Gopi discovered the same when he saw students *employing their incorrect understanding* of basic operations like subtraction, while solving simple problems. Kanchana attributed her students' errors to several causes – lack of comprehension, incorrect use of mathematical language and a difficulty in visualising geometry problems, to name a few. And Michael came upon an interesting realisation: he initially drew a connection between the quality of work turned in and the state of mind of the student – by attributing randomly done work to a disinterested state of mind. However, he later revisited this assumption when he saw that students made more errors when they began to write complex sentences. This, he finally discerned, was actually a sign of students having acquired the confidence to attempt writing complex sentences.

Sometimes, the manner in which a question is framed also lends itself easily to errors. Movshovitz-Hadar et al. (1987) examined 300 students' answer sheets on national mathematics tests in Israel. They analysed repetitive errors and found that these could be traced to certain editorial practices, which, when altered, resulted in fewer errors. (At times, these editorial changes were as seemingly insignificant as interchanging the letter 'l' for the numeral 1; putting connecting words together on the same line, without breaking them up into two lines; or avoiding the insertion of superfluous information, which could confuse the student.) Prerna experienced something similar when she tried answering a question that her student had fumbled with – and realised, to her shock, that even she could not answer it, as she had not framed it clearly enough! This resulted in her adopting the practice of always answering the questions that she expected her students to attempt, even before expecting it of them.

Thus, aware and attentive teachers gradually develop a nuanced understanding of why students commit errors through such explorations. As their understanding of the causes of the students' errors deepens, so do their pedagogies. Consequently, they can design customised strategies for tackling respective challenges.

Given the packed day of most teachers, the likely demand of long durations of time for such work is the first deterrent – even for an otherwise interested teacher. This leads us, therefore, to the next question.

How much time does a teacher need to invest?

Being the first and foremost consideration for any busy teacher, a summary of the actual time invested by the four teacher-researchers of this compilation is shown in Table 2.

Table 2: Time invested by the four teacher-researchers

Name	Time invested on a weekly basis	Duration of the action research
Prerna Pradhan	With students – only during class hours, as per the time table With facilitator – Eight half-hour meetings online spread over four months	Four months
Michael Moses	With students – mostly during class hours, occasionally outside class hours for struggling students With facilitator – 14 half-hour meetings online spread over four months	Four months
Gopalakrishnan	With students – mostly during class hours, occasionally outside class hours for struggling students With facilitator – Six meetings online only for the purpose of documentation, spread over six months	15 months
Kanchana Suryakumar	With students – mostly during class hours, occasionally outside class hours for struggling students With facilitator – Six meetings online only for the purpose of documentation, spread over six months	Two years

A couple of teachers (Michael and Gopi) did invest extra time towards evaluation of students' work initially, but this decreased as the research progressed; and they either dropped that way of evaluating or simply became more efficient at it. (The interested teacher can glean a rough estimate of the extra time that he/she may initially need to invest from Table 2.)

Strategies Developed by the Four Teacher-Researchers

Each of the four teacher-researchers adopted different routes to find the strategy that worked best for their own context. By their very definition, Pierce and Kalkman (2003) emphasise that learner-centred practices are fluid as they respond to the needs of individuals. Thus, here too, the four teacher-researchers carved out their unique paths that were best suited to their own situations.

Since these pathways have been described in detail in each chapter, a broad overview is given in Figures 1, 2, 3 and 4.

As can be seen from Figures 1, 2, 3 and 4, all the teachers followed the usual Plan-Act-Observe-Reflect cycle of action research. Their individual strategies varied within this framework; a few highlights are as follows:

✦ Prerna chose to adopt simple strategies to help her students identify and overcome errors, given the young age of her students.

✦ Michael expected his (older) students to follow a checklist to identify their errors, but soon found that this assumed that the student understood what constituted an error. If his students were aware of this, he then realised, they would not have committed those errors! Therefore, he later found it meaningful to indicate the type of error made by students in a broad region of the page, and then push them to *think about the exact location of the error.*

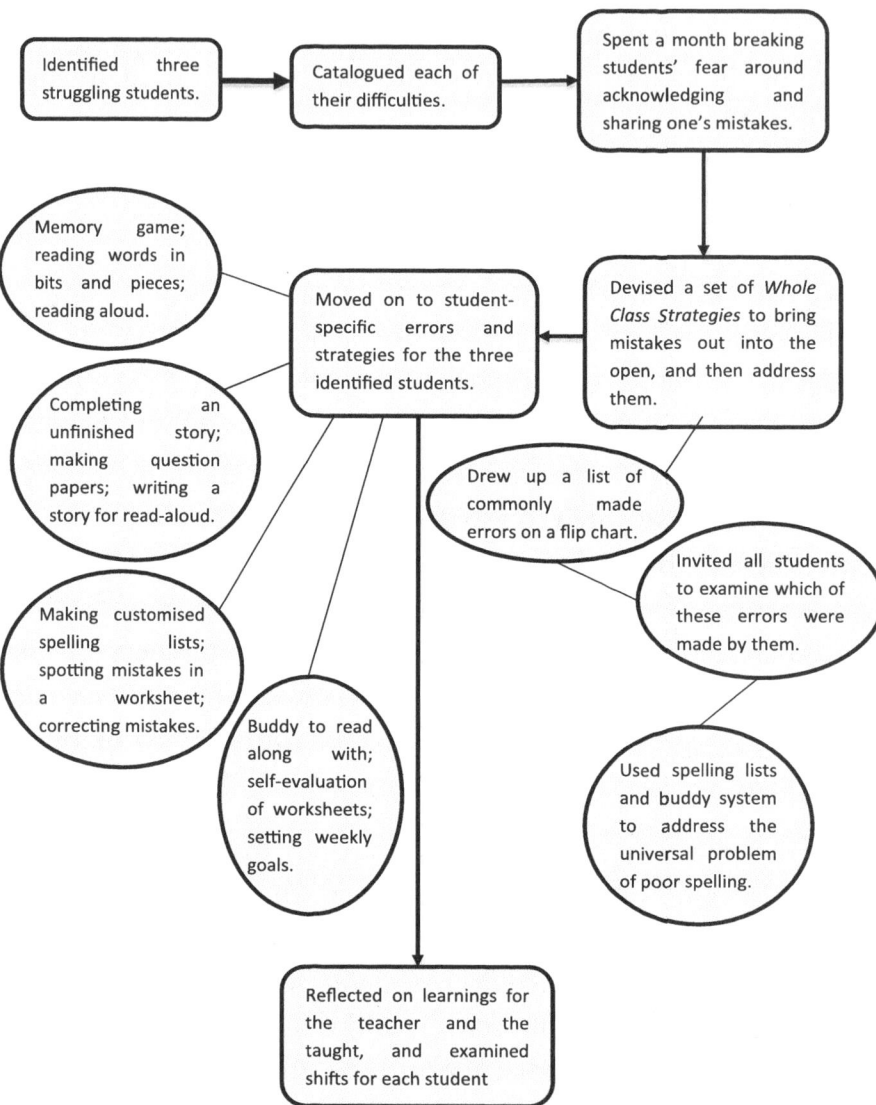

Figure 1: Flow chart of Prerna Pradhan's research

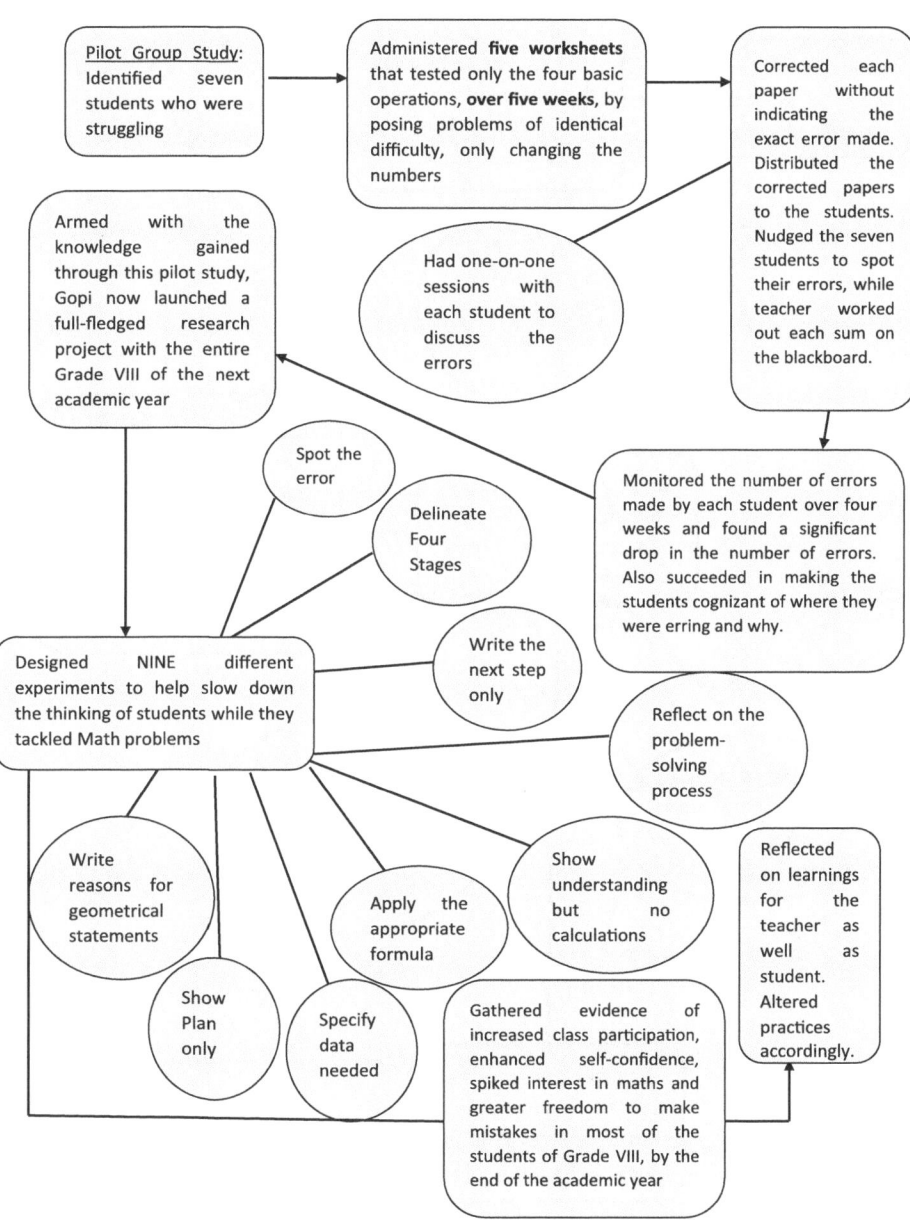

Figure 2: Flow chart of Gopalakrishnan's research

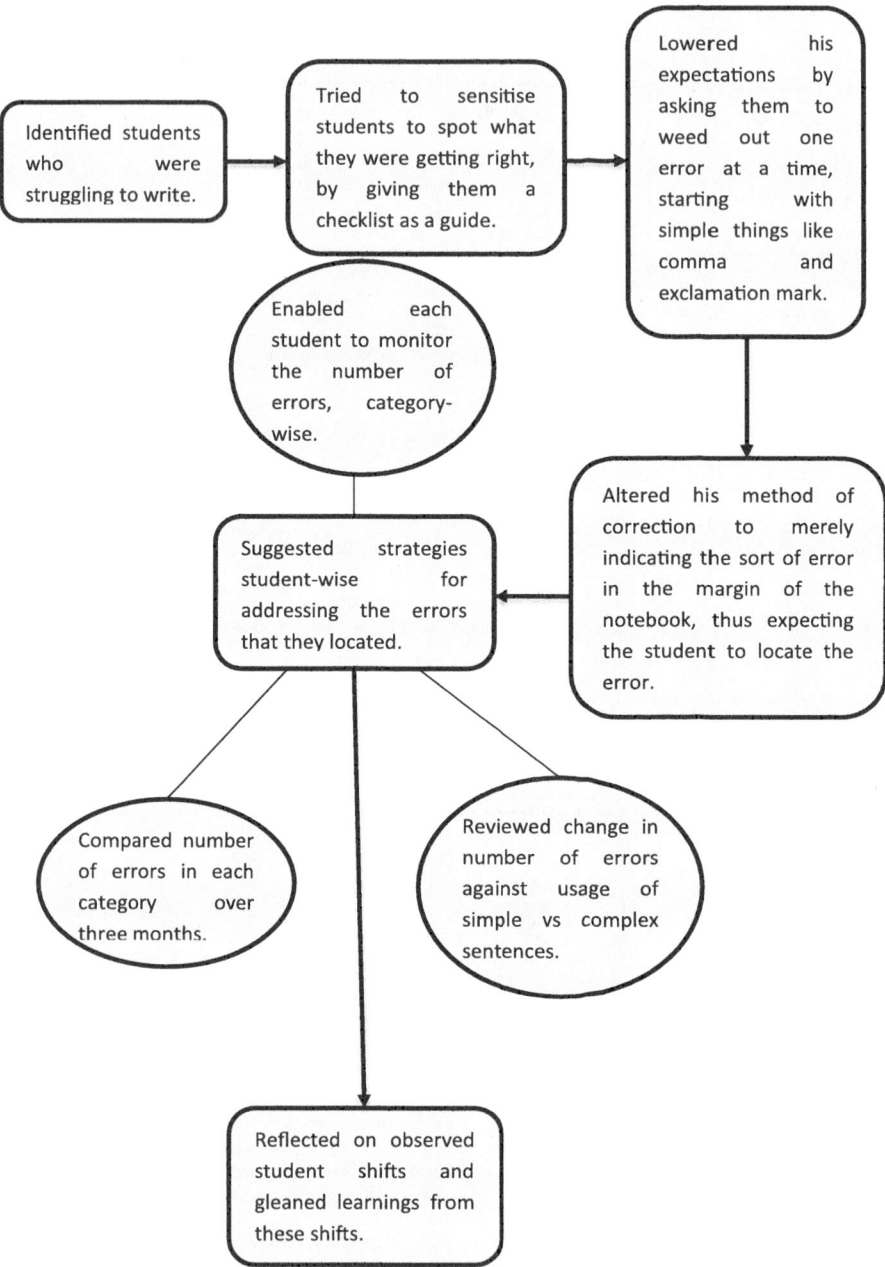

Figure 3: Flow chart of Michael Moses' research

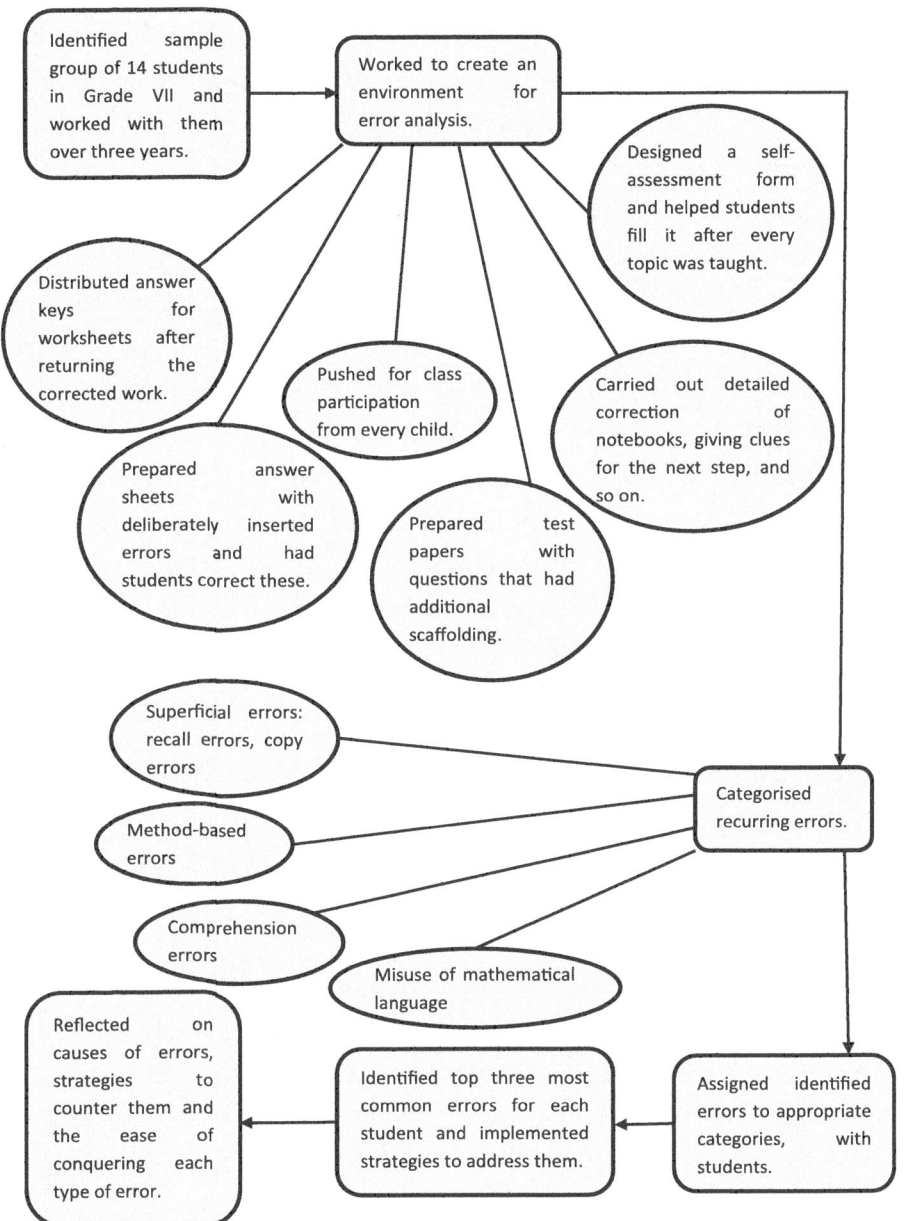

Figure 4: Flow chart of Kanchana Suryakumar's research

✦ Gopi designed a variety of experiments to sensitise his students to the multiple ways in which a mathematical problem could be thought about. His efforts were directed towards getting his students to see how data could be viewed; or how formulae needed certain data, and when it would be deemed appropriate to use a particular formula. As he went along, he designed experiments that helped them slow down and think deeply, keeping his central goal in focus all through, viz. to get into the mind of a student. He reaped rich rewards when his students began to see that mathematics was not just a problem-solving exercise, but *a way of thinking*.

✦ Kanchana designed a rubric for helping students carry out self-assessment. She supplemented this effort with careful and detailed correction of students' work, and participated in the analysis of their error patterns until they became adept at it themselves. The insights that her students gained are evident from her research paper.

Sequence of Steps for a Teacher-researcher to Carry out Such Research

Broadly, the following are the steps for an interested teacher (Figure 5 illustrates a suggested road map):

1. As already described, the first challenge for a teacher-researcher would be to explore how the act of making mistakes is held in each one's mind, by opening up the subject for unfettered discussion. It is only after a climate has been created for enquiring into mistakes (without feeling ashamed or judged) that the research can begin.

2. Once such an atmosphere prevails (and this is hard work, with no prescriptive process), the next step would be to scaffold the students' efforts to identify and categorise their errors. There are several rubrics available in the research literature

for an interested teacher to use in class. The focus of this book is not to survey available rubrics (which can easily be found on the Internet) but to show how teachers can develop their own rubrics. Just as each of these four teachers arrived at their own way of categorising and identifying errors, it is best if teachers work their way through the error patterns that surface in their class, so as to customise a rubric that suits their unique needs.

3. Having empowered students to diagnose their repetitive error patterns, the teacher would then need to help them strategise conquering these errors, preferably one at a time. As experienced by the four teachers here, this is seldom a linear progression – as many complexities can surface through this journey. Here, it may be pertinent to point out how Michael tried various strategies, and then decided to stick to one approach (indicating the broad location of an error, but expecting the student to zero in on its exact location). He decided to try out this approach for a sustained period before switching to another, and this decision stood him in good stead, as his account reveals. The teacher-researcher, therefore, has to strike a balance between trying out various methods and sustaining one method.

4. Through this entire process, it is unlikely that the teacher will not feel compelled to reflect, and it is even less likely that the student will not reflect. As discoveries are made both by the teacher and the student about causes of errors and the frequency of certain errors or error patterns, the way the student's mind engages with the subject at hand will reveal itself. The teacher will uncover prior assumptions about the students' understanding or the degree to which a concept needs to be opened up before students can begin to get comfortable with it. The teacher will then also feel the need to adapt his/her pedagogy to suit the thinking of the

students. An intertwining of the student's thinking and the teacher's teaching will organically ensue as a consequence of such research.

Role of Principal

It is critical that a teacher-researcher is supported by the administration of the school in some way or the other, if the teacher is to carry out research of any sort.

The four teacher-researchers enjoyed the support of the Heads of their schools, and so were able to accord the time needed for such research. During the year of conducting research, Gopi was actually given fewer classes to take, so that he could focus on his research. Prerna and Michael had their Skype sessions with the facilitator slotted into their daily time table by the school administration, thus avoiding the need for them to work outside school hours to plan and monitor their research. Kanchana was fully supported by the Director of her school in this research, by way of brainstorming as well as actual inputs. In fact, the Director worked during the summer vacation with one student who needed remedial instruction, and periodically shared her learnings with Kanchana.

What Are the Options for a Teacher Who Does Not Wish to be a Researcher?

There are several shorter routes for a teacher who feels disinclined to engage in long-term research (or is unable to get the support of the Principal to carry out such research), and yet, is keen on drawing out the reflective learner from the students. While there are no short cuts to deepening reflection, a teacher can certainly employ numerous triggers – which, if found to be sufficiently interesting by either the teacher or students, can lead to organically evolving research. A few such triggers are outlined as follows:

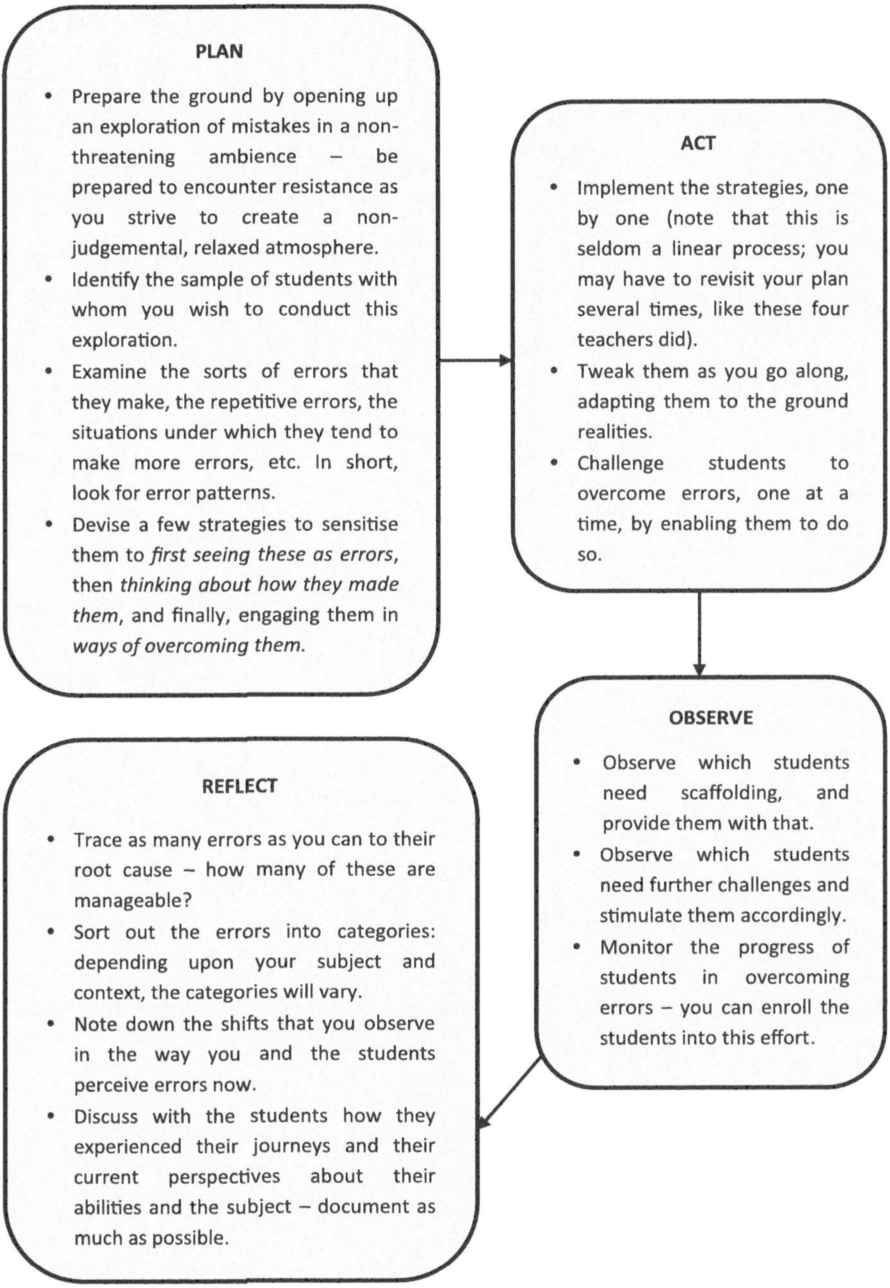

PLAN

- Prepare the ground by opening up an exploration of mistakes in a non-threatening ambience — be prepared to encounter resistance as you strive to create a non-judgemental, relaxed atmosphere.
- Identify the sample of students with whom you wish to conduct this exploration.
- Examine the sorts of errors that they make, the repetitive errors, the situations under which they tend to make more errors, etc. In short, look for error patterns.
- Devise a few strategies to sensitise them to *first seeing these as errors*, then *thinking about how they made them*, and finally, engaging them in *ways of overcoming them*.

ACT

- Implement the strategies, one by one (note that this is seldom a linear process; you may have to revisit your plan several times, like these four teachers did).
- Tweak them as you go along, adapting them to the ground realities.
- Challenge students to overcome errors, one at a time, by enabling them to do so.

OBSERVE

- Observe which students need scaffolding, and provide them with that.
- Observe which students need further challenges and stimulate them accordingly.
- Monitor the progress of students in overcoming errors — you can enroll the students into this effort.

REFLECT

- Trace as many errors as you can to their root cause — how many of these are manageable?
- Sort out the errors into categories: depending upon your subject and context, the categories will vary.
- Note down the shifts that you observe in the way you and the students perceive errors now.
- Discuss with the students how they experienced their journeys and their current perspectives about their abilities and the subject — document as much as possible.

Figure 5: Suggested roadmap for teacher-researchers

Closing the loop

In the usual rush of 'covering the syllabus' and preparing students for the end-of-year examinations, a very important step of closing the loop is often missed. While lessons may be planned carefully, and transacted by the teacher with even greater care, the important step of going over the corrected answer sheets and figuring out *why and where mistakes were made* is frequently missed. The dashed lines in Figure 6 depict the missing step in closing the loop.

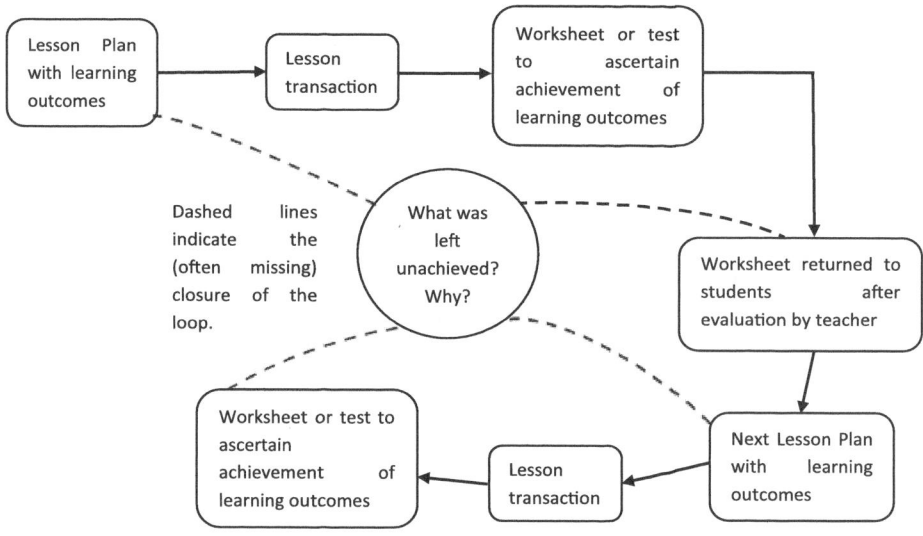

Figure 6: Lesson planning, transaction and evaluation of achievement of learning outcomes

When teachers insist that students examine their evaluated work and *redo the incorrectly done work correctly,* there is some chance of closing the loop. However, this step is often ignored in the rush to move forward with the prescribed content, or because the teacher cannot afford to spend time checking the corrections done by each student again. The result is that the gaps in learning simply get carried forward, and accumulate towards the end of the year. In order to avoid investing a short duration of time in closing the loop, enormous amounts of time are later required to address cumulative learning gaps. In India, this often translates into a spate of hurried remedial classes, tuitions or, worst of all, selective study of only those portions that are expected to be assessed in the final examination. True learning clearly gets a back seat by this time.

At the very least, therefore, the simple practice of regularly discussing with the entire class the corrected worksheet, test, or examination is something that any teacher would do well to invest time in. Normally, when corrected answer sheets are distributed, students are more engrossed in noting their scores than in figuring out why they made the errors that they did. If a teacher can spend just one period at the end of every evaluation discussing the common errors and helping students see why they fell into these traps, it can prove to be beneficial to both the teacher and the students. Chances are that during such a discussion, ambiguously worded questions will also be brought to the notice of the teacher, and avoidable errors will come to the attention of students – in short, they will begin to see where they are prone to making mistakes. This investment of one period for each corrected worksheet is bound to reap rich dividends in the long run.

Articulating shifts in thinking

In their classic book *Making Thinking Visible*, Ritchhart, Church and Morrison (2011) offer a rich array of methods to provoke and express thinking in students. Among these is the simple practice of getting students to write down what they 'used to think' about a certain concept or subject on which the day's lesson is built, and then, after transaction of the lesson, what they 'now think' about it. Simple as this sounds, teachers who employed this strategy unearthed powerful shifts like the following:

✦ Students began to monitor themselves and notice their own habits that pulled them away from focussed learning.

✦ Some students began to believe in themselves more than before, as they saw the falsity of their earlier beliefs in their lack of capability.

✦ Students' perception about writing changed from regarding it as a boring activity to being fun, because it lends itself to free expression.

Getting nine- and ten-year-olds to reflect

'What about younger children? In what ways can third and fourth graders, for instance, be enabled to reflect on their learning?' An attentive reader or interested teacher may wonder. (The youngest class showcased in this book are fifth graders – Prerna's sample.)

The following is an example from a school which conducted a reflection exercise with children in Grades I to VI.

Vidhya Nagaraj, Principal, Delhi World Public School, Bangalore (Karnataka), was keen to find out how much the younger learners at her school were absorbing at the end of each lesson. As she confessed,

Most often, when teachers ask if the students have any doubts, or if they have understood the concept that was taught, very few students may ask questions. Several students hesitate, feel shy or refrain from asking for various reasons like lack of self-confidence, low self-esteem or invalidation of their question by the teacher. Worse, they may even think that asking doubts would invite a reprimand from the teacher for not paying attention in class.

Teachers, too, often find it difficult to gauge whether the entire class has truly understood the concept taught. To compound this further, it is seldom that the lesson taught in class is experienced by the learner as being directly linked to everyday life.

Today the biggest problem faced is that students – and sometimes, teachers – might not see the connect between what is being taught in class with the real world. As a result, the students don't see the point in learning whatever they are learning and they think that it is irrelevant. But when we have them do a review of their learning and write out what they are going to apply in the real world – this makes learning more meaningful. When they see this connect between what they learn and the real world, learning becomes deeper and more impactful.

With this in mind, she instituted the following practice in Grades I to VI: after a lesson is taught and students' understanding is assessed by the teacher in a worksheet, each student is asked to review the learning at the end of the answer sheet. The review includes three parts:

1. What I clearly understood …
2. I still have doubts in …
3. I can apply this learning in …

The above three pointers give students an opportunity to reflect and articulate their positions. Figure 7 illustrates a few examples of their responses.

If such things are possible with young children, how much more can be achieved with adolescents?

An interesting experiment

It is pertinent to describe another interesting experiment that was conducted by Ramakumar, a teacher who taught physics to eleventh graders at a school that follows the Central Board of Secondary Education (CBSE) curriculum. While designing their course, he tried to bring in a good mix of self-driven learning as well as teacher-delivered content. Thus, even as Ramakumar taught them physics from the prescribed textbook, he encouraged them to do some browsing on the Internet for certain concepts, threw open the option of reading other books for some topics and even invited them to deliver a seminar – over and above the curricular requirements like answering worksheets and performing experiments in the laboratory. Not surprisingly, meeting these demands was not equally easy or difficult for all the students in the class. Depending on their motivation levels and ease with reading, browsing the Internet or speaking before the class, each one rose to the challenge differently. At the end of the year, he had them write out their own report cards, which was perhaps a first-time exercise for all of them. Therefore, he scaffolded this effort by giving them a broad framework to follow.

The teacher deliberately gave them the opportunity to step back and view their efforts and delivery as dispassionately as possible. Students wrote about their efforts and learning over the year in the third person. As each student reflected on the degree to which they had met the various demands of the physics course, their self-critical tone and honesty is evident even in the small sample shown in Figure 8.

Some of them gave themselves an overall grade, too. The most surprising outcome, Ramakumar confessed, was that without exception, every grade accorded by the student was lower than what he, the teacher would have given! Here again, the common notion that left to themselves, students will be easy on themselves is turned on its head. This is another device that provokes reflection in the student. Depending on the maturity of the learner, this practice can be far more compelling in drawing the student's attention to existing lacunae than can traditional rituals like withdrawing privileges, reprimanding the student or issuing a sharp note to the parents.

Reflection Can only Enrich the Class

It seems so self-evident – even trite – to say that reflection can only enrich a class. And yet, there is a need to state it – for, in the rush to tick things off a list, or achieve high scores, how often are teachers and students pausing to reflect? How often are school administrations seeing the need to allow the time and space for such reflection to occur?

Several options have been laid out here for the reader to explore. The intent of this book is to bring to the attention of the reader the immense potential embedded in mistakes to draw out metacognition and reflection in a student. If it were to even trigger a reflective journey in the classrooms or homes of some of the readers, the intent would have been fulfilled.

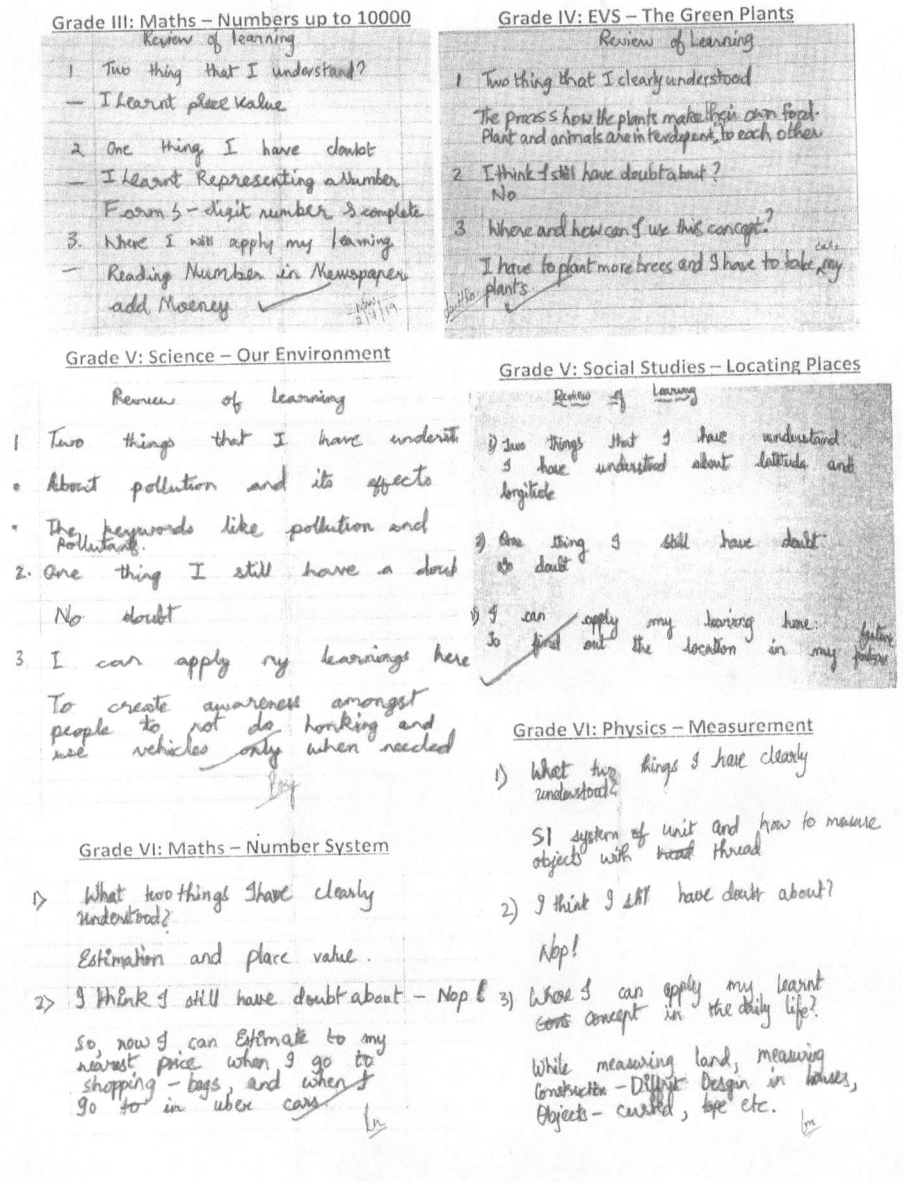

Figure 7: Students' review of their learning

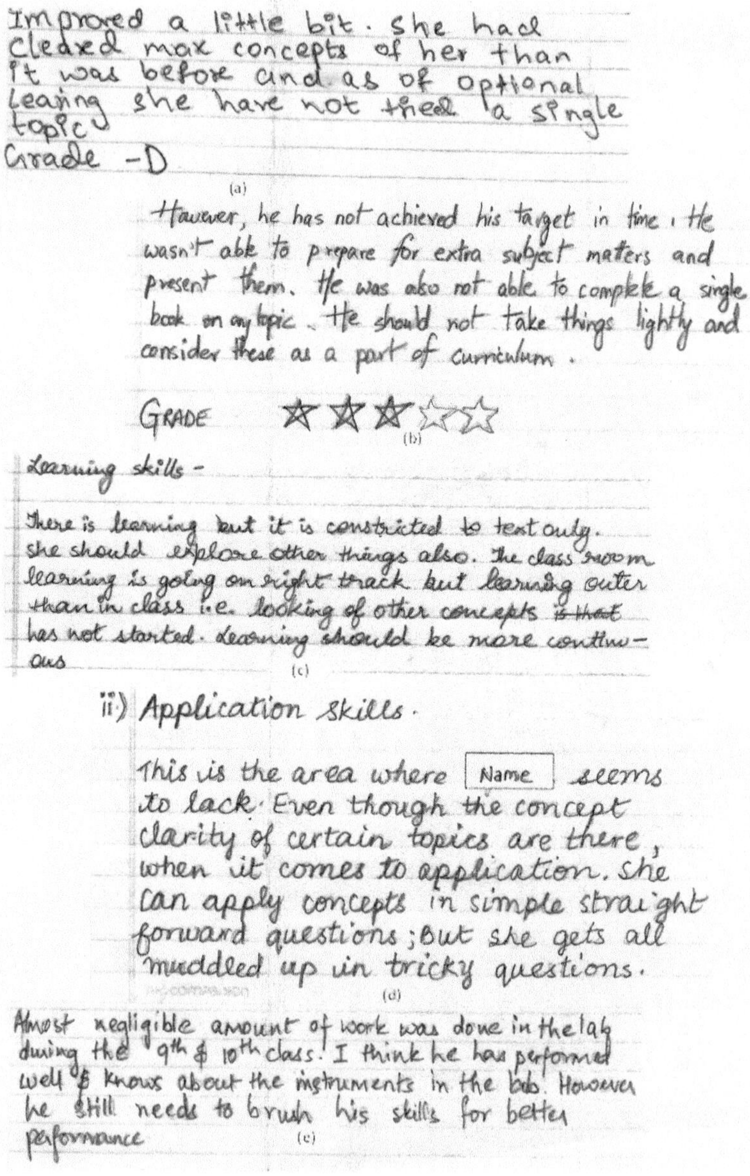

Improved a little bit. She had
cleared max concepts of her than
it was before and as of optional
leaning she have not theer a single
topic
Grade -D

(a)

However, he has not achieved his target in time. He
wasn't able to prepare for extra subject maters and
present them. He was also not able to complete a single
book on any topic. He should not take things lightly and
consider these as a part of curriculum.

GRADE ★★★☆☆

(b)

Learning skills -

There is learning but it is constricted to text only.
She should explore other things also. The class room
learning is going on right track but learning outer
than in class i.e. looking of other concepts is that
has not started. Learning should be more continuous

(c)

ii) Application skills.

This is the area where [Name] seems
to lack. Even though the concept
clarity of certain topics are there,
when it comes to application. She
can apply concepts in simple straight
forward questions; but she gets all
muddled up in tricky questions.

(d)

Almost negligible amount of work was done in the lab
during the 9th & 10th class. I think he has performed
well & knows about the instruments in the lab. However
he still needs to brush his skills for better
performance

(e)

Figure 8: Scanned images of five Grade XI students' self-evaluation of their efforts to learn physics

References

Ball, D. L. 1991. 'What's all this talk about "discourse"?' *Arithmetic Teacher* 39(3): 44–48.

Bouvier, A. 1987. 'The Right to Make Mistakes'. *For the Learning of Mathematics* 7(3): 17-25.

Fennema, E., M. L. Franke, T. P. Carpenter and D. A. Carey. 1993. 'Using Children's Mathematical Knowledge in instruction'. *American Educational Research Journal* 30: 555-583.

Fennema, E., T. P. Carpenter, M. L. Franke, L. Levi, V. R. Jacobs and S. B. Empson. 1996. 'A Longitudinal Study of Learning to Use Children's Thinking in Mathematics Instruction'. *Journal for Research in Mathematics Education* 27: 403–434.

Gattegno, C. 1954. 'Mathematics and the Child. III: The Use of Mistakes in the Teaching of Mathematics'. *The Mathematical Gazette* 38(323): 11-14.

Movshovitz-Hadar, N., S. Inbar and O. Zaslavsky. 1987. 'Sometimes Students' Errors Are Our Fault'. *The Mathematics Teacher* 80(3): 191-194.

Pierce, Jean W., and Deborah L. Kalkman. 2003. 'Applying Learner-Centered Principles in Teacher Education'. *Theory into Practice* 42(2): 127-132.

Ritchhart, R., M. Church and K. Morrison. 2011. *Making Thinking Visible: How To Promote Engagement, Understanding and Independence for All Learners.* San Francisco: Jossy-Bass

Schleppenbach, M., L. M. Flevares, L. M. Sims and M. Perry. 2007. 'Teachers' Responses to Student Mistakes in Chinese and U.S. Mathematics Classrooms'. *The Elementary School Journal* 108(2): 131-147.

Swearingen, M. E. 1952. 'When Children Make Mistakes in Spelling'. *Elementary English* 29(5): 258-262.

ENDNOTE

For any suggestions or clarifications, interested teachers (readers) may contact the teacher-researchers at the following email addresses:

Name of teacher	Email address
Prerna Pradhan	prerna.pradhan@taktse.org
M. Gopalakrishnan	truthalonefrees@gmail.com
Michael Moses	kalimpongmoses@gmail.com
Kanchana Suryakumar	kanchana.suryakumar@live.com

 **Neeraja Raghavan** is Founder Director of Thinking Teacher (www.thinkingteacher. in), and author of several books and research papers, the most recent being *Teaching Tales, Learning Trails*, co-edited with Vineeta Sood and Kamala Anilkumar (Notion Press, 2018). She holds a doctorate in chemistry from Princeton University, and has more than two decades of teaching experience (in both mainstream and alternative schools) as well as in research, with a couple of years as Vice Principal/ Principal of schools. Her current focus is on teacher development through action research and reflective practice. She enjoys reading philosophy, writing poetry, listening to music and sketching.

Also, by the same author:

THE FIVE DAY FEST (Kindle Edition Only, 2018)

TEACHING TALES, LEARNING TRAILS (with Vineeta Sood and Kamala Anilkumar) (Notion Press 2018)

THE REFLECTIVE TEACHER (with Vineeta Sood) (Orient Blackswan, 2015)

ALTERNATIVE SCHOOLING IN INDIA (with Sarojini Vittachi) (SAGE, 2007)

CURIOUSER & CURIOUSER (Full Circle, 2005)

I WONDER WHY (Children's Book Trust, 2004)

I WONDER HOW (Children's Book Trust, 2004)